# God's Plan
## for Spiritual Battle

### Victory Over Sin, the World, and the Devil

Russell M. Stendal

RANSOM
PRESS
INTERNATIONAL

*God's Plan for Spiritual Battle* - Russell M. Stendal
Edited version of *The Beatitudes*, by the same author.
Copyright © 2013,2019
Second Edition Published 2019
*Cover by Amber Burger*
*Edited by Sheila Wilkinson*

Printed in the United States of America
Ransom Press International
4918 Roosevelt Street
Holywood, Florida, 33021

Paperback ISBN: 978-0-931221-12-5
eBook ISBN: 978-0-931221-13-2
*10  9  8  7  6  5  4  3  2  1*
*Available where books are sold*

# Contents

# Dedication

I Dedicate this book to my wife, Marina, and the four wonderful children that God has given us. Our marriage in 1980 marked a watershed in my spiritual life as the Lord used Marina to smooth many rough edges off me and placed our lives on a steady course towards attaining more and more of His Blessing. She has proven to be a wonderful helpmeet and has had a great impact on the contents of this volume.

The birth of our daughter, Elizabeth Jean (we call her Lisa), in 1982 marked another turning point in my life. About that time, I began to feel a strong call of God to walk in victory (with clean hands) before Him. At first, I thought God was asking me to do the impossible, but from the time of Lisa's birth, I felt God's grace renewed in my life. Elizabeth literally means "to whom God is the oath" in Hebrew, and I've discovered since then that God is faithful to His Word with Himself (with the power of His presence), in the lives of those who take Him seriously.

Sixteen years ago, I was in a great dilemma trying to name our second daughter. The baby was almost a month old and still didn't have a name. I felt an impulse to put down the baby-name books and get out my concordance. I found a beautiful name for our lovely girl using the Greek word for truth. The birth of Alethia Joy, meaning "the joy of the truth," was a great milestone in my life. The Lord had been teaching me the full meaning of the verse *and you shall know the truth, and the truth shall set you free* (John 8:32). As Christians, the truth is our weapon, and if used in submission to the will of God, brings great deliverance, victory, and joy.

Ten years ago, the Lord granted me one of the desires deep within my heart with the birth of Russell Martin Jr. The birth of my son marked the initial gathering of material that has culminated in this volume. The baby has given my wife and me great joy as he develops, learning to sit, crawl, and talk (when I edited the first edition of this book in 1993, Russell Jr. was just learning to walk). The birth of little Russell marked a great change of course in our ministry. For more than seven years, we stopped preaching to multitudes to spend quiet time with the Lord. This led to being the editor of over fifty books and two Bible editions (the Reina Valera 2000 in Spanish and its counterpart, the Jubilee Bible in English).

Our second son, Dylan Andrew, was born in 1999, and then the Lord put us back into public ministry on the radio, and in person (now in a new dimension).

As I have learned more and more about parenting, I have been able to identify a little more with how God the Father feels as He trains and develops us as His sons. As I have learned more about being a husband, I have been able to identify with the desire of our Lord Jesus to return for a victorious bride (church) without spot or wrinkle. For this reason, I also dedicate this book to all the true sons of God who form part of the "bride without spot or wrinkle" for whom our Lord will soon return.

– *Russell M. Stendal, August, 2002*

# Introduction

## "First the worker, then the work."

By this phrase, Cameron Townsend, "Uncle Cam," the founder of the Wycliffe Bible Translators, meant that God wanted to bring Christian workers into a complete consecration to the Lord. Then God could bless and multiply their Christian work based on the biblical standard of love – love for the lost and love for other workers. By this, the whole world should know that the workers and the work were of God (1 John 3:14). The hardest part of this task was helping the worker into a right relationship with the Lord. After that, it was a relatively easy matter to add hundreds and even thousands of believers to the Lord.

My wife and I worked hard for many years under the most demanding primitive conditions. The Lord did many wonderful things for us and opened previously closed doors to the Kogi tribe in northern Colombia. We endeavored to walk in the Spirit and be obedient to His will. All four of our children grew up in the nurture and admonition of the Lord, and now with their spouses are serving God with us in Colombia.

In 1975, after 13 years, we left the Wycliffe Bible Translators, with the blessing of the director, and labored to win rural Colombians and Indians to the Lord. This was more complex than we had imagined. It was not hard to bring them to a superficial commitment, but to see real, changed lives, as the New Testament teaches, was difficult indeed. We had many disappointments, as even some of our workers did not continue victoriously. Somehow, imperceptibly, our own consecration began to slip from the 100 percent commitment and dedication to the Lord with which we had entered Colombia in 1964. Discouragement set in.

But God is faithful and did not leave us in that condition of despair. On August 14, 1983 our oldest son, Russell, was kidnapped by Marxist guerrillas. Russell's coworker in a new Family Reconciliation Ministry called me. "I'm so sorry to tell you, Chad, that Russell has been kidnapped," he sadly told us.

Russell had flown his plane to Caño Jabon, a small town on the edge of the jungle, to help the local people set up a fish marketing co-op. Right then, as I finished talking with Ricardo, the Lord showed me that God had just "called" a missionary to the communist guerrillas.

All his life, Russ had been very active, running about as though he were connected to a high-voltage electric line. He was capable of accomplishing a great many things, but the spiritual results were not commensurate with the amount of physical effort he was expending. He was too busy to take the time in quiet meditation with the Lord so that he might draw close to the heart of God and be more effective.

All of a sudden, as a prisoner in the jungle with a nylon rope around his neck and shoulders, tied to a tree, he had a lot of time to think. The Lord simply sat him down for 142 days and began to teach him the things he needed to know to be completely consecrated to God and to hear His voice.

Meanwhile, the Lord was doing the same with the rest of our family and coworkers. My wife, Patricia, almost wore out her knees in prayer. We all covenanted together to walk as close to the Lord as we could, and He brought us all much closer together in love. We trusted that God in His great mercy might hear and answer our prayers for Russell if we met the conditions of James 5:16: *The effectual prayer of the righteous is very powerful.*

On the other hand, we had to recognize that if God in His infinite wisdom had selected my son to be a martyr, then we would accept His will. Most of the apostles gave their lives, and this is the highest honor the Lord can bestow.

Finally, after almost five months, Russell was released. We all discovered that God had done a profound work in each of our lives, perfecting us to a much higher plane than we had ever dreamed of experiencing. The Lord multiplied our ministry a hundredfold. Churches all over Colombia, the United States, and Canada had been praying for Russell's release. Now they opened their doors for ministry. The small Family Reconciliation Ministry grew to be a National Reconciliation Ministry, extending the gospel to the drug mafia and the guerrillas. Radio ministry began to flourish.

One day I asked the Lord why Russell had received such a great anointing for ministry, and the Lord showed me that He was restoring to the church a class of anointed preachers called "Confessors." During the great persecution in the days of the early church, the Lord not only had martyrs, of whom it was often said, "The blood of the martyrs is the seed of the church," but the Lord also had "Confessors." These were those who had maintained a good testimony under much persecution and torture. They were tried by the fire and found faithful and true. Many were maimed or blinded, but did not deny their Lord. After they were proven to be faithful, the Lord ordained their release, and a great unction and power followed their ministry for the rest of their lives.

In the following book, Russell has distilled the most important fruits of the truth the Lord has shown him during the last ten years, starting with those 142 days in the jungle, "First the worker, then the work."

– *Chad Stendal Bogotá, Colombia August, 1993*

# Preface

Let me ask you a question. What section of Scripture is most relevant to your Christian life? Between the Old Testament and the New Testament of the Bible, most of you would probably pick the New Testament. If you were to consider what the most important part of the New Testament is, I think most Christians would probably single out the four gospels, recognizing that the life, death, resurrection, and ministry of our Lord Jesus Christ is the most important part of the New Testament.

Out of the four gospels, if you were to pick three chapters that sum up and synthesize the message that Jesus Christ came to leave with us, the Sermon on the Mount is the prime candidate. At times, it has been called the Constitution of the kingdom of God, the Magna Carta of the Christian church, and the Little Gospel. There have been more books written on the Sermon on the Mount than on any other Scripture text. Entire libraries could be filled. The Sermon on the Mount has challenged Christians ever since it was given. The proclamation of the Beatitudes by Jesus Christ at the beginning of his public ministry marked the climax or watershed of moral teaching. After His message on the kingdom of God, proclaimed both by His lips and through His very life, death, and resurrection, this world has never been the same. Human history was divided in two: before and after Jesus Christ.

The first few times I read the Sermon on the Mount, I sensed that it contained something important; but for many years, Jesus' Beatitudes and His Sermon on the Mount seemed as if they had been written in code. I knew they contained something special, but I couldn't put my finger on it. In confirmation class, I was taught the Lord's Prayer, the Beatitudes, and the Ten Commandments, but I couldn't figure out why I had to memorize all these things. It seemed like an unbelievable waste of time. I never understood the message God was trying to reveal to me, as I'm sure many of the thousands and thousands of young people who have been forced to memorize the same things never really understood its purpose.

One day I was driving up the road from Miami to Minneapolis. As we were going through Chattanooga, Tennessee, I turned on the radio and heard a preacher I didn't know, but what he said stuck in my mind. He said, "How in the world can we expect to have a deep revival when we are dealing with such a superficial generation?" Do you want a deep revival? Would you like to see a deep revival? Would you really like to see the power of God move in our present society?

Well then, we need to search for God. We need to uncover our hearts before Him. We need to seek Him in a very deep and profound way. God will not give His valuable treasures and powerful gifts to people who just want to be mediocre, superficial Christians, to people who are trying to do the minimum to go to heaven. That's a terrible position to be in. God is looking for people who will seek Him in spirit and in truth and who are willing to go His way no matter what.

The great heroes of the faith all went through trials and tribulations. God told Abraham to leave his family, friends, and home town and travel to a land He promised to give him. After Abraham obeyed, God promised him a son, an heir, through whom all the families of the earth would be blessed (Genesis 12:2). Twelve years after the miraculous birth of Isaac in his old age, Abraham was called upon by God to sacrifice his son who was most dear to him. When Abraham passed that test, the Bible says that Abraham believed God, and it was counted to him as righteousness and that Abraham is the father of those who have faith. Faith (believing God) is closely linked to obedience in the Scriptures. If we truly believe God, then we should also be willing to obey Him. If you don't desire to obey God, you really shouldn't read any further in this book about the Beatitudes of the Sermon on the Mount.

I say this because I don't want to have a part in bringing someone under worse condemnation than they already deserve. If you are not going to act on revelation of truth, it might be better for you not to know any more about it because then your responsibility will be less. If you listen to the Sermon on the Mount and begin to understand Jesus' message, but do not apply it or begin to practice it or implement it into your life, there is a great and grave responsibility that comes with refusing to act on your knowledge of revealed truth.

Jesus' ministry was preceded by John the Baptist, who was a typical prophet in many ways, but not typical of many preachers today. He preached a simple message, and it was this: repent and prepare the way for the coming of the Lord. If you are truly repentant, your life should change, and there should be visible fruits of repentance. John said that the axe has been laid to the root of the tree (Matthew 3:1-11). Time is running out; judgment is at hand. That was for the Jews, the ones who rejected this message, those who rejected Jesus, whom John the Baptist was announcing. They didn't have long to wait before their entire nation was uprooted and destroyed, and the survivors dispersed all over the known world.

John the Baptist was heralding the end of the age of the Old Testament (the old covenant), the end of the worship in the temple at Jerusalem. A new age, the age of the church, was dawning. In this age, God promised to live in a temple not built with human hands. God's temple is now us, His people.

*Know ye not that ye are the temple of God and that the Spirit of God dwells in you? If anyone defiles the temple of God, God shall destroy that one; for the temple of God is holy, which temple ye are* (I Corinthians 3:16-17).

I am convinced that we are now drawing near to the end of the age of the church. The city of Jerusalem is once again in the hands of the Jews after almost two thousand years of being trampled by the Gentiles (Luke 21:24). Our Lord Jesus Christ's return is getting closer and closer. God is getting ready to move again and do something special, something new. He desires to raise up a people, a victorious people who have washed their robes in the blood of the Lamb, who have left their own plans and ambitions to one side and have become willing to do things His way, no matter what the cost.

There is a cost involved in following the Lord; but it is a price that we must pay voluntarily, of our own free will. Jesus is not a terrorist. He's not like the communist guerrillas I met who point machine guns at people in order to get them to do what they want. He doesn't do things that way. If we want to try our own way and implement our own ideas, He lets us go ahead with them. We are free to discover the disastrous consequences of going our own way. Tragically, much of Christianity today is wandering around in the wilderness of man's good intentions and has never been able to enter into the promised land of God's rest where God fights our battles, where God opens the doors, where God leads the way, where God miraculously breaks the power of the enemy, and where we come along behind Him and possess the land in His Name.

As we look at the world today, organized Christianity is being thrown for loss on most fronts. We complain about the secular humanism that is running rampant in the schools of North America. We complain about the news media. We complain about Hollywood. We complain about all the sexual perversion and the abortions that are going on across this continent. We complain about the drug traffic. We complain about violence and insecurity. The list of our complaints goes on and on. Why should it be that the power of the enemy, the power of rebellion and the power of sin are so strong as to displace Christianity? How can this be? Iniquity should not be able to displace the presence of God; the presence of God should be able to displace the darkness.

What I believe it boils down to is that many of the people who are calling themselves God's representatives, calling themselves members of God's church, calling themselves part of the body of Christ, really, truly are not manifesting Jesus Christ through their lives, their attitudes, or their actions. They are not fighting the battle according to His plan. What many call Christianity is in reality humanism, religious humanism, and it will not, cannot, stand against the enemy. Religious persons and organizations are doing their own things in the name of God, expecting God to bless them, and He won't. He can't. God has some powerful things to say about it. Let us read just one of them.

> *And he cried mightily with a strong voice, saying, Babylon the great is fallen, is fallen, and is become the habitation of demons, and the hold of every unclean spirit, and a cage of every unclean and hateful bird. For all the Gentiles have drunk of the wine of the wrath of her fornication, and the kings of the earth have committed fornication with her, and the merchants of the earth are waxed rich through the power of her delicacies.*
>
> *And I heard another voice from the heaven, saying, Come out of her, my people, that ye not be partakers of her sins, and that ye receive not of her plagues. For*

*her sins have reached unto the heaven, and God has remembered her iniquities* (Revelation 18:2-4).

God is talking about the fall of "Mystery Babylon." In the course of biblical history, Babylon has symbolized many things, all the way from the ancient (Old Testament) kingdom we know as Babylon to the early Christians calling pagan Rome Babylon, to Babylon being a type of apostate (prostituted) Christianity which has been defiled by the man-made, economic, and political systems of the world under Satan's control. In a nutshell, the roots of Babylon are in human selfishness which always brings mankind under bondage to the enemy. Babylon is a type of the religious humanism that attempts to conduct the church of God according to the ways of the world, the world that according to the Scriptures is at enmity with God (James 4:4).

Are we going to implement God's kingdom our own way, this world's way? Or will we do it God's way? The Sermon on the Mount talks about doing it God's way. So often, when we receive good Bible teaching, we say "amen" to the preacher and leave church saying, "That message was right on." Then we go home and pigeon-hole it in the Babylonian file system in our minds; we put it right in its niche, right on top of the Babylonian foundation on which we have built our lives and human organizations, and then wonder why we are not seeing God's power and glory in our lives and in our churches.

Some of you can remember back to a day when God was moving, back when there was a real, authentic move of God, and maybe you are wondering why it isn't happening any more. In a certain sense, we cannot decree when God should move; He is not our servant; we are His servants. But in another sense, if we are not where God wants us to be, and He wants to move, He will pass us by and find someone who will do it the way He wants. That's tragic. Throughout history, He has passed different nations and peoples by. He dearly wanted to be received by His people, the nation of Israel. I believe the offer He gave to the Jews was a genuine offer. He wanted to bring the millennium in right then and there and begin to bless the world through the Jews, but they rejected Him. And out of the ashes of that rejection, He instituted the Christian church.

And the Christian church has a mixed record as we look back over history. There are huge sectors of the world where Christianity has made few inroads. There are Muslim countries in the world today where the Christians can be numbered on the fingers of one hand. These enemy fortresses have hardly been touched by Christianity. Or worse yet, there are places where Christians have gone, only to be defeated again and again and again. But what really bothers me is that enemy power, strength and resources are growing right in the midst of what used to be Christian nations in Western Europe, United States, and Canada.

The apostle James says that when we know that which is good and don't do it, that it is sin (James 4:17). I think one of the great sins of the Christian church has been our failure to oppose the enemy, failure to oppose evil according to God's way and according to God's plan.

I want to look at the Beatitudes, not just in the light of something you can define as "Isn't this wonderful? Aren't they logical? Doesn't it all fit beautifully?" but in the light of a battle plan, in the light of "This is something that we can begin to practice and implement in our lives, so that we will be able to stand in the day of evil that is coming. So that when everything else is shaken, we won't be shaken." The Bible says that everything that can be shaken will be shaken (Hebrews 12:26-27). Do you want to stand? Do you want what you believe to be your Christian faith to fail the minute there is some adversity? Or do you want to develop godly character in your life that will stand against any attack of the enemy, so that the storm can rage, the winds howl, and the floods rise, yet your house stands firm because it was founded on the rock. Jesus says,

> *Therefore, whosoever hears these words of mine and does them, I will liken him unto a prudent man, who built his house upon the rock; and the rain descended, and the rivers came, and the winds blew and beat upon that house, and it did not fall, for it was founded upon a rock.* (Matthew 7:24-25)

The Greek word for house, oíkos, has an extended or figurative meaning. It can mean house, or it can mean household. Jesus was talking about a house that represents our household or family. He was saying that if we put His teachings into practice, our families will be founded on the Rock, which is Himself, and we will not be shaken no matter what kind of storm is brewing around us.

We are living in dangerous times. I find Christians who didn't believe in a literal devil or in a literal hell, and suddenly some of their children were almost sacrificed to the devil by literal Satanists. I meet people who didn't believe that when the Word of God speaks out against homosexuality and promiscuity, that it was a message for us in our present day and age. Now some of these same people are dying of AIDS, others are witnessing the death of their children or their friends.

There are incredible forces of darkness at work today. Satan is in the business of bringing as many people down with him as he can. He realizes that his time is short. He's not playing games. Satan plays for keeps. When he louses somebody up, and that person dies that way, it's for keeps. People are really being lost, people who could even be from your own family. The stakes that we are playing for are incredibly high. We are talking about the priceless lives and souls of men, women and children.

We are definitely in a spiritual battle for the hearts and souls of those held in bondage by the enemy. I hope and trust that the truth God has revealed to me from the Beatitudes will have as great an impact on your life and ministry as it has had on mine.

This truth was not revealed to me in an abstract manner, but through the lives of men and women of God who have had a great impact on my spiritual formation. To give due credit to all those whom God has used in my life would require that I write a separate volume, but I wish to mention one very special person that God placed in my life.

This person is my father, Chad Stendal, who laid the spiritual foundation (total commitment to the Lordship and authority of Jesus Christ) for everything that I would accomplish later in life. My dad is still my best friend, and I have called upon his God-given wisdom, insight, and discernment for help and correction throughout the writing of this manuscript.

There is a sense in which this book has been coming together for the past ten years, ever since a memorable incident in early 1983. I had been in a very frustrating type of ministry since 1974 when my brother and I homesteaded a ranch in eastern Colombia with a vision to train, send out, and support Christian workers to evangelize Indian tribes. I was on a rare trip to Bogotá, the capital city of Colombia, and was lodged in the San Diego hotel downtown. It was clear to me that our ministry was in a stalemate; we were not winning over the enemy in eastern Colombia. Armed gangs of violent drug traffickers and groups of Marxist guerrillas were threatening most aspects of our work. But what really bothered me were the inconsistencies and defeats I was experiencing in my own personal life.

After spending some time alone in prayer in my hotel room on the seventh floor, I picked up the phone and on an impulse called an old friend of our family. Ricardo was bubbling over with joy from a revelation he had just received from the Lord while ministering in Venezuela. In a few minutes, he met me at the San Diego and began to share it with me. The message was none other than the Beatitudes of the Sermon on the Mount. The Lord met with us in such a way that we both made a commitment to dedicate the remainder of our lives to preaching the Sermon on the Mount. Little did we know what the full ramifications of our meeting that afternoon would be.

The message of the Beatitudes turned out to be like the scroll that was given to the prophet Ezekiel (and later to the apostle John in Revelation): it tasted sweet, but was bitter to stomach. I no sooner started preaching Jesus' message than I was put to the test. I was kidnapped and held hostage for almost five months. The Lord allowed me to prove the Beatitudes under extremely difficult circumstances so I could preach them with authority.

Since that time, God has opened many doors for ministry in seemingly unlikely or impossible circumstances. I have learned a great deal about God's plan for battle as I have followed the Lord into public schools, universities, army barracks, prisons, churches, and even back into the guerrilla camps. I have learned some of God's secrets for victory and revival that I now feel great urgency to share in print.

I love a good fight. And when unjustly attacked, I have learned to seek the leading and guidance of the Holy Spirit and retaliate by overcoming evil with good. There's a huge difference between a peacemaker and a pacifist.

This battle plan, gleaned from the life and message of Jesus, has been on my heart even before I was kidnapped by terrorists in 1983 and held hostage under extreme conditions. Since then, thousands of missionaries, pastors, and Christians have been kidnapped, murdered, or forced to flee from their places of ministry in rural Colombia.

Many of those who chose to remain in the path of ever present danger have rallied around this message. A thriving underground church is beginning to multiply in a huge area about the size of North Korea in the south and east of this country where Bibles, church buildings, formal ministry, and even house meetings have been prohibited for more than 25 years.

Severe persecution in rural Colombia has served to bring real Christians together, identify the true church, and cleanse believers from corruption so that the promises of God can be fulfilled.

– *Russell M. Stendal, November 2009*
*When a man's ways please the LORD, he makes even his enemies to be at peace with him* (Proverbs 16:7).

*And they have overcome him (Satan) by the blood of the Lamb and by the word of their testimony; and they loved not their lives unto the death* (Revelation 12:11).

A little church in a small town invited me as a guest speaker several years ago. Unknown to me, this congregation in western Minnesota was going through some problems. These difficulties had the potential to harm the church. The pastor, not knowing what to do, decided to bring someone in from the outside to preach, hoping that God would use an outsider who knew nothing of their problem to address their need. After a lot of prayer and reflection, he chose me. The pastor called me and was overjoyed when I confirmed that I was available for the date he had in mind. He even put an ad in the local paper announcing that I was going to be there Sunday morning and evening.

Everything was going fine until the Saturday night before I was scheduled to speak at this church. A dear friend phoned and wanted to know if I could be in Winnipeg, Canada by 10:00 a.m. Monday to appear on a television program. Years before, at the start of my ministry, I had promised the Lord that I would not cancel a small meeting to do a larger one somewhere else. I did not want to be a respecter of persons or churches and I understood that many times small things are more important in the Lord's work than the big things are. But now I forgot my promise to the Lord.

Sunday morning, I preached in the little church. The sermon went well, and even though I didn't know anything about the difficulties they were having, I hit on their problem. The pastor was really excited and enthused until I told him after lunch that I needed to be in Winnipeg by 10:00 a.m. the next day. I wanted to get out of doing the evening service and leave immediately. "No, don't do that." he said, "Take a nap; you can sleep in my bed. Do the evening service and then drive all night if you need to."

"No, I need to be in good shape when I arrive in Winnipeg." I was thinking of being on TV and did not want to arrive with circles under my eyes. "No, I've got to go. There's this big opportunity to be effective for the Lord on television."

So I climbed in the car and started to drive (at least I thought I started to drive) to Winnipeg. I headed north on a US highway and soon arrived in Montevideo, Minnesota where there is an unusual triangular intersection. It was raining very hard, and my alternator belt started to slip. I was getting a discharge indication because it did not want to run the lights, the blower and the wipers all at once. I found an old abandoned service station where I could drive in out of the rain and try to tighten the belt. But when I came back out on the road at this funny triangular intersection in the heavy rain, I went the wrong way. I turned south instead of north. So, because I had to make that appointment in Winnipeg, I was driving as fast as I could go, but in the wrong direction.

After two or three hours of driving, the discharge light came on again, so I pulled off the road and found a better place to work on the car. I pulled my blue jeans on, got out a crowbar, slid under the car, and really tightened up that alternator belt so it could not slip any more. Then I went to make a phone call. The area code on the public phone was from either the extreme south of Minnesota or the northern part of Iowa. I was chuckling to myself, "Imagine the crazy nut that brought a pay phone from Iowa and installed it all the way up here in northern Minnesota."

I was still chuckling about that when I got back in the car

and drove out to the main highway. A sign indicated north or south, so of course I pulled out north, going the right way now. I drove and drove and drove for another couple of hours. Finally, I started thinking that I should have hit the interstate a long time before. Where in the world was I? I pulled over at another intersection and got my map to find out where I was.

I could find no such road in northern Minnesota, so I had to look all over the map. Finally, I found that I was thirteen miles south of Clarkfield, which was where I had started, and I had been driving all afternoon. "Oh no, it's almost time for the evening service." I thought, "And I'll be driving right through Clarkfield. What if someone sees me? They'll think I was a liar when I said I had to go to Winnipeg. I better not go through the town; I better turn left at this intersection and go out to Interstate 29 and up to Winnipeg through the Dakotas."

I turned left on the county road that intersected the US highway and drove about three or four miles when there, before my eyes, I saw a pay phone out in the middle of a cornfield – just a cornfield and a pay phone sitting beside the road. When I saw that phone, I knew the Lord was speaking to me to pull over, so I picked up the phone, called the pastor and said, "If you still want me to speak, I'm available." The pastor was just leaving his house for the church, and I said, "I haven't got time to explain, but if you still want me to share, I can be there."

He said, "Yes, come on down."

So, I returned to the church and arrived several minutes late. The song service was in progress, and I had to speak in my greasy blue jeans. I told them how I had spent the afternoon. That message turned out to be very effective and hit the nail right on the head in terms of the error of some of the people. The church was reconciled and went forward in the Lord. I got back in the car and drove all night to Winnipeg and appeared on television the next morning. After the show, I conked out in the middle of the television studio offices, so I had to tell them what had happened too.

When our hearts are set on serving the Lord and doing what He wants, even if we make a mistake and get the 'bit in our teeth' or become confused, the Lord can still intervene and help us. I thought I was going to Winnipeg, but I had told the Lord that above and beyond everything else I wanted to serve Him and He was in charge of my life. So, if I wanted to drive up and down the state of Minnesota, that was my problem, but He was going to securely help me arrive at the right place at the right time. As we become sensitive to the Lord, and as we learn to walk in His Spirit, we don't have to beat our heads against the wall so much, and it becomes easier and easier to follow Him.

God offers us complete security in Jesus Christ if we will only submit to His authority. He is the only one who can overcome the enemy, and He is offering to dwell inside each and every one of us.

The story of Gideon (Judges Chapters 6 and 7) gives perspective to what we will study in this book. Throughout the Bible, an Old Testament story will contain a type or reference of Jesus Christ (in parable). King David, for instance, typified Christ in many ways. Joseph typified Jesus, as did Joshua and many others. Gideon is an outstanding example. He was the youngest son in the least important family in Israel. The angel of the Lord appeared to him and called him to lead His people to victory. Gideon checked it out; he wanted to make sure it really was the Lord. He didn't want to go following after any spirit that was talking to him. He genuinely wanted to know if this was God, and he resolved his doubts by putting out fleeces. But once he was sure that God was really talking to him, he began to follow orders wholeheartedly.

Gideon blew the trumpet and announced the message: God's people were in bondage, and they needed to overcome the enemy. You remember the story – thirty-two thousand men answered the trumpet call to fight in the Lord's army against Midian. Then God said to Gideon, "Tell the ones who are afraid to go home." Twenty-two thousand men went home and left Gideon with only ten thousand men to face a vastly superior enemy force.

When it comes to engaging the enemy, when it comes to standing for the Lord, when it comes to really taking on enemy strongholds, when it comes to getting the victory over sin in your own life, what is your attitude? Are you afraid to try? Are you a person who wants to be saved and no more? A person who wants to do the minimum required for salvation in the future with no desire to be saved from the habitual bondage of sin here and now?

How can we have assurance of salvation and eternal life through the power of God in the future if we are not experiencing the power of God in our lives at present to save us and deliver us from the bondage of habitual sin here and now through the presence of His life within us? Remember that the simplest definition of sin according to the Word of God is "going our own way, instead of going God's way."

*There is a way which seems right unto a man, but the end thereof are the ways of death* (Proverbs 14:12).

*For the wages of sin is death, but the grace of God is eternal life in Christ Jesus our Lord* (Romans 6:23).

*Jesus said unto him, I AM the way, the truth, and the life; no one comes unto the Father, but by me* (John 14:6).

One day, a dear friend of ours (a clergyman) brought a man to us who was frothing at the mouth, gritting his teeth, rolling his eyes, and screaming demonic curses. With difficulty, he got him to the door of the house, and we occupied ourselves in dealing with the situation. I turned around after a few seconds to greet our friend, wondering why he wasn't helping us, but he was gone. He brought that guy to our doorstep and took off running as fast as he could go.

I'm sure that is how those twenty-two thousand would-be warriors of Gideon's were. "Are you afraid?" "Yes!" "Well then, go home." And Gideon didn't have to say another word to them; they all disappeared.

That left ten thousand men, and you know how the story ends; God only chose three hundred. He asked Gideon to have them pass before him and drink water. The ones that laid down their weapons, lay down on the bank, and scooped up the water with both hands, God said were unfit for His army. But the ones who had their weapons in one hand and were ever watchful for the enemy while they lapped the water with their other hand, those were the ones He picked, the ones that really meant business. The water might typify the Holy Spirit – for our comparison, let's assume that it does.

We're talking about ten thousand Christians attempting to be filled with the provision of God's Holy Spirit, yet out of that army of ten thousand, 9,700 of them were no good for facing the enemy. Why? Because they were interested in taking the water of the Holy Spirit (the power, gifts, and blessings of God) only for themselves and for filling their own needs. They were not really interested in their weapons, or aware of the enemy. They were just sitting there fat, dumb, and happy; too stupid to really understand the danger that they were in.

As I travel and speak across the country, I see churches full of people who are using the anointing and gifts that God has given them to get things for themselves; they are not fully aware of the enemy or of the great spiritual battle raging around us.

They are not alert and interested in getting the job done; they're not interested in pressing on and winning the victory.

God cannot use them in His army because if He tried to put them in the front lines of the battle, they would be wiped out. So rather than lose them, He sends them home too. Another reason He cannot use them in the battle is that when He wins the battle, they'll think they did it, and they'll take the credit for it and become so proud that Satan will trip them up.

So, the thirty-two thousand men who joined the army of God were reduced to three hundred. God gave them a strange, strange plan. He told them to take three hundred pitchers and three hundred torches and to cover the torches with the pitchers. Then God told them to take three hundred trumpets and get into position inside the enemy camp in the middle of the night.

Have you ever heard of such a crazy plan? It's the only plan I can think of in the Scriptures where the light is covered up. The Sermon on the Mount says we are to let our light shine and be like cities on the hill top (Matthew 5:14-15). But here the Angel of the Lord is talking about covering up the light until the proper time. If we are really going to get the victory, if we are really going to win the battle, we have to follow our orders. God has chosen to work through His people. God has chosen to use people like you and me. If God can't get us, His people, to do what He wants done when He wants it done, how is He supposed to win the battle? At the end of the book of Isaiah, He says He couldn't find anybody to help Him with what He was going to do, so He rolled up His sleeves and did it Himself. But it's talking about bringing terrible, terrible judgment upon the inhabitants of the earth. Do we want that? (Isaiah 63:5).

Gideon's three hundred men got down into the midst of the enemy camp and broke their clay pots, exposing the light. I think the clay pots are a symbol of the earthen vessels that we are. God isn't interested in polishing and smoothing and making bigger and better earthen vessels. If we are going to win the victory, the clay pots have to break to let His light shine out. We are still trying to keep our clay pot intact while at the same time we are trying to let our light shine; it's a contradiction; we can't have it both ways. If the light is to shine through us the way He wants it to, our clay pot must break or the light will always be hidden under the bushel.

You and I need to be willing to let Him break us of everything He does not want. We must be willing to allow the Spirit of God to put to death the deeds of the flesh (Romans 8:13). Only then can God's light shine forth (through us) in a way that will overcome the enemy.

The enemy became confused; the enemy did not know what to do. At the same time, Gideon's men blew their trumpets, which is the call of the message: the living Word of God that only He can put on our lips which will rally the people of God for battle and strike uncontrollable fear into the hearts of their enemies. The Bible says that the enemy (the Midianites) turned upon themselves; Gideon didn't really have to kill all his enemies; they took care of most of it for him.

Then, when the Midianites were on the run, the Bible says that the 9,700 men that were sent home, the twenty-two thousand men that left because they were afraid, and some guys that never showed up to be in the army in the first place all came running out of the bushes and helped finish off the enemy and chase them out of the land. The entire nation of Israel was delivered, probably several million people.

So we do not have to be a majority. It only takes a few men and women, or even children, who are interested in building on the right foundation, which is the Lordship of Jesus Christ. It takes total surrender to Him as Master and Lord and willingness to give up everything and follow Him; the willingness to say, "Lord, break me, make me into what You want me to be." This is the battle plan.

I'm not much of a theologian, but I've told some of the

theologians I know that I believe there is only one essential doctrine that is worth fighting for. That doctrine is the Lordship of Jesus Christ. He's right; He's the only one that is right. It's not my opinion vs. your opinion vs. someone else's opinion, or this doctrine vs. that doctrine. It's what He thinks about it, and how He feels about it, and what He wants done about it. That's where it's at. If we look at the body of Christ from this perspective, He will draw true believers together to Himself and lead them to victory (Genesis 49:10).

The Scripture is clear: It says *unto Him shall the gathering of the people be.* If we are trying to unite people under any banner other than the Lordship of Jesus Christ, we will ultimately fail, and Satan will bottle up the church again. It's not a question of whether the Protestants are better than the Catholics or the Baptists vs. the Presbyterians or the Pentecostals vs. the Charismatics. Is Jesus Christ the Lord? Is He the King? Are we willing to act on that no matter what the cost?

I have known people with their theology totally warped, with theology that would make your hair stand on end if they told it to you, but who were sold out to Jesus Christ. Jesus will work with people like this, and He'll straighten them out in the end if they have submitted to Him and placed their lives under His authority. Not only that, but when we give Him authority over us, He gives us security. This is how Gideon won the victory. This is how Jesus intends to win the victory over evil and purify all of the things that are wrong in our personal lives, in His church, and in the world that we live in today.

The victory is available, and in a certain sense it is free, because Jesus Christ has already won the victory. But in another sense, it will cost us everything we have because to be a part of His army, to be part of Him, we need to be willing to leave everything else behind. *For whosoever desires to save his life shall lose it, and whosoever will lose his life for my sake shall find it* (Matthew 16:25). This is the only way to be truly satisfied.

So, imagine that you are a Pharisee who has been standing in the (spiritual) desert beside the Jordan River, listening to the preaching of John the Baptist. You have come under conviction from the Holy Spirit, and you have decided you want to repent from the dead works of your organized religion. You want to turn from going your way and doing your own good works; now you want to go God's way. John the Baptist has baptized you in the Jordan River, and Jesus Christ is sitting up on the mountain; you have followed Him there, and now you are going to listen to what He has to say.

> *And seeing the multitudes, he went up into the mountain; and when he had sat down, his disciples came unto him; and he opened his mouth and taught them, saying, . . .* (Matthew 5:1-2).

The first thing you now must decide is are you one of the disciples who left everything to follow Christ, or are you one of the multitude who is looking on? Some of those people were probably wondering, "Boy, John the Baptist is a fiery prophet, and they say this one is even better. He does all kinds of miracles. I wonder what He's going to say. He's probably going to say, 'Unless you repent, you're all going to be cast into the depths of hell and burned up.'" They were probably expecting literal fire and brimstone. And what they got was *Blessed are the poor in spirit, for theirs is the kingdom of the heavens . . .*

A paraphrase of this verse in Aramaic (which is probably the language Jesus taught in, according to the Peshitta text which is still used by the Eastern Orthodox Church) could be: Blessed are the poor in pride for they and only they have God as their King. The word "poor" here is not a word that means you have a little bit of something, like a little bit of pride or not too much wrong, but we'll still decide what is right. We'll pay God our tithe, but we're still going to decide what to do with the 90 percent that is left over. We'll go to church on Sunday, but we're still going to decide what to do with the remaining six days. We want the blessing of the Lord, but we are not willing to pay the price of returning the knowledge of good and evil back to God.

The tragic thing about this is that it is not the path to restoration; it is not the way to re-obtain the blessing of God. There is a catchy word going around in Christian circles: "renewal." Exactly what is it that we are trying to renew? Many good things God doesn't want to renew. There are man-made divisions, doctrines, traditions, and barriers that we try to renew which God may want to dismantle so his church can truly be restored.

God wants to restore us. Restoration is different from renewal. Renewal can be superficial; restoration goes down as deep as it needs to get things back on the right foundation. The path to genuine restoration of the church requires that we be willing to dismantle some of our good human ideas which are really an abomination to the Lord (if they were never ordained by God in the first place), so He can start over and complete what He originally intended (making us into men and women of integrity by conforming us to His image). Renewal can mean polishing up our hypocrisy so that it looks nice. God does not necessarily want to renew our human plans, traditions, programs, and religious machinery that we have attempted to implement in His name; He wants to restore us to proper fellowship and communion with Himself. He only wants to renew those things that He deems right and were developed on the right foundation in the first place.

The word "renew" is used less than a dozen times in Scripture, the first usage being the renewal of the kingdom of Israel under King Saul, which was a disaster (I Samuel 11:14). In half a dozen positive uses of the word "renew" in Scripture (such as in Romans 12:2), the word is carefully qualified by the context to mean the renewal of that which sovereignly comes from God.

On the other hand, the verb "to restore" is used over one thousand times in the Word of God and contains connotations of completion, purification, and a return to wholesomeness (peace). It is also related to the Hebrew greeting "shalom," which means peace (wholeness). This peace can only come from a right relationship with the Prince of Peace, not just from an absence of war.

Blessed are the poor in pride, those who choose to relinquish their pride, those who choose to have God divest them of their pride, for they and only they have God as their King. Do you want to have God as your King? Do you want to belong to Him? Do you want Him to say, "Yes, those are My people. They belong to Me."

Or do you want Him to look at you and say, "Well, they did all kinds of wonderful works; they prophesied and cast out demons in My name, but I never knew them. They never did the will of my Father in heaven. They belong to themselves. They belong to the world and to the prince of this world. Depart from me, you workers of iniquity" (Matthew 7:22-23).

It's going to be one way or the other; there is no in-between course. Do you want to be able to stand in the presence of the Lord and look Him square in the eye and have Him say, "Well done, good and faithful servant. You have been faithful in a few things. Come, receive your inheritance because now I am going to put you over many things." Do you really want this to happen?

LET US PRAY:

*Heavenly Father, help us to understand the difference between doing things Your way and doing things our own way. Lord, please help us to understand the importance of allowing You to be sovereign. You have created us in Your image, and You have made us sovereign over our own little will with the ability to decide whether we are going to go Your way or whether we are going to go some other way. That's really all our will can do. In our own strength and our own understanding, we are not capable of going Your way even when we try. It takes Your grace; it takes Your Spirit; it takes Your anointing; it takes You in control to be able to make us into what You want us to be: to be able to train our hands for war, so we can stand against the enemy.*

*Lord, I pray we might be willing to relinquish our good ideas and be willing to relinquish the things we consider to be rightfully ours: our time, money, talent, families, possessions, profession, whatever it may be that is holding us back from obtaining Your best. May we be willing to return totally what was taken from You in the garden. May You be God, not only of what is wrong, but also God of what is right. May we be willing to say, "Lord, I have this wonderful idea, but if You don't think it's a good idea, then I'll drop it. If You've got a better idea, then I want Your best."*

*Lord, I don't want to wander around in the wilderness of my own good intentions. I don't want to be confined in the cage of my own mediocre ideas when Your best is spread out on a table before me, when I can dine in Your presence and go forth under Your anointing and win Your victory. Lord, may we understand the difference between the Babylonian systems of this world and Your way. May we understand that time is short, and the need is great. Fill us with Your feelings, power and anointing and raise up an army that can stand against the enemy and defeat him in Your Name, under Your leadership. Please help us to obey You down to the smallest detail. Help us comprehend what is at stake.*

*Lord, as You are looking on and searching our great nation, trying to decide what to do, whether to let this nation reap what it has sown and go down the drain into destruction and chaos, as has happened to so many different countries and peoples in the history of this world, or whether when You look down at this nation, You see men and women totally surrendered to Yourself who are willing to stand in the gap and pay the price to face the enemy in Your Name, according to Your way, so You can win a tremendous victory, lift the oppression of the demonic forces, and deliver this nation from the hands of the enemy.*

*Lord, may we be found worthy in Your sight to be called Your sons, that You might look on us and say, "They're mine. They belong to Me. I bought them. In spite of all their human weaknesses and failures, they really want Me to be in charge. They really want to be under My authority, they really want to do things My way, so I'm going to bless them. They're going to stand victorious before their enemies. Their enemies will come from one direction and flee in seven directions. No weapon that is formed against them is going to prosper. The enemy will lie in ambush and shoot arrows from the shadows, but I'll set My sights on the enemy. I'll shoot My arrows at him, and he will not escape and will not be found."*

*Lord, we know You can change the fate of our country.*

*For, behold, the day comes that shall burn as an oven; and
all the proud, and all that do wickedly shall be stubble;
and the day that comes shall burn them up, said the
LORD of the hosts, that it shall leave them neither root nor
branch. But unto you that fear my name shall the Sun of
righteousness be born, and in his wings he shall bring saving health; and ye shall go forth and jump like calves of the
herd. And ye shall tread down the wicked; for they shall be
ashes under the soles of your feet in the day that I make,
said the LORD of the hosts. (Malachi 4:1-3).*

John the Baptist came as a type of Elijah to prepare the way
for the ministry of the Lord. In hindsight, we see that he
came to herald the end of an era; the Old Testament age had
ended. Most of the Jews rejected the ministry of the Lord. They
turned on Him. They said, "Crucify Him! Let His blood be upon
us and our children." (Matthew 27:23-25). This is exactly what
happened. The Christian church was planted by the Holy Spirit
in the ashes of the Jewish rejection of Christ, and the gospel
was then offered to the Gentiles. Only in recent years has the
nation of Israel come back to the Holy Land, after almost two
thousand years of blindness and continued rejection towards
the Gospel of Jesus Christ (their Messiah).

The Bible says that Jerusalem will be downtrodden by the
Gentiles until the times of the Gentiles be fulfilled (Luke 21:24).

Now, with the Jews back in Jerusalem, it is clear we are approaching the end of the age of the church. Every day that passes comes a little bit closer. We do not know exactly when, but we do know that the Lord is at the door again, and we are waiting for His second coming. This is the hope that all believers have.

The prophet Malachi reported that. Therefore, we now say blessed are the proud and even those that work wickedness are prospered. I did a film on the cocaine traffic, and one scene showed some of the mansions the drug traffickers are living in. School principals and people in the educational system said, "Don't show that to the kids. If they see those mansions, they are going to want to live like that, and they'll all want to be drug traffickers!"

We are living in a day and age when the arrogant are called blessed, when the people who can find a way to beat the system, to traffic in drugs, to cheat, lie, or steal to get ahead, are looked at in many quarters with a certain amount of respect. But the Lord says there is a day coming when He is going to act, and the tables are going to turn.

There is a day coming which will be like a furnace, and all the stubble will be burned up. Only the gold, silver, and precious stones will be left. Only that which we have done in obedience to the call of Jesus Christ will have lasting, eternal value. The prophet Malachi says that for those of us who fear His (God's) name, a new day will dawn, a new age of righteousness. We will go forth on that day, and the wicked will be like ashes under our feet. *Behold, I send you Elijah the prophet before the coming of the great and terrible day of the LORD: and he shall convert the heart of the fathers to the sons, and the heart of the sons to the fathers, lest I come and smite the earth with destruction* (Malachi 4:5-6). This is complete destruction or anathema such as what happened to Jerusalem in AD 70.

Family reconciliation is essential to God's plan. It's at the

God has created each of us with a conscience so we can know if we are pleasing God or not. The more we obey God and respond to what we know is right, the more sensitive our conscience becomes.

Now look at the next beatitude. *Blessed are those that mourn, for they shall be comforted.* The Greek word for mourn, *pénthos*, is very important. It is the term that was used for mourning the dead. It can also mean a passionate grief that leads to action. Those who mourn are those who die to their own way and live to follow Christ, their master. This leads to some very hard choices. Worldly pursuits that used to provide fleeting pleasures must be renounced. Jesus tells us that *No man can serve two masters.* Those who truly surrender to God and submit to the authority of Christ will grieve at the status of the world around them. They will renounce ill-gotten gains, as well as the pursuit of worldly power, prestige, and pleasure even if it causes them great grief at the time.

Those who renounce their own way and the ways of the world to take up their cross and follow Christ will be comforted. The Greek word, *parakaléo*, translated "comforted" has a wide range of meaning. It can mean anything – calling for aid, beseeching God in prayer, being exhorted, being encouraged (or even won over to a given plan), and being comforted in times of sorrow. This is the same root as the word used in the gospel of John for Comforter (Holy Spirit).

When we choose to give up the ways of the world by renouncing everything that belongs to the kingdom of darkness, God responds by giving us the down payment on our inheritance in Christ: He sends us the Comforter. The Holy Spirit will exhort and encourage us in the way of the Lord. He will convince us of the truth.

*But the Comforter, which is the Holy Spirit, whom the*

*Father will send in my name, he shall teach you all things and bring to your remembrance all the things that I have said unto you* (John 14:26).

*And ye shall know the truth, and the truth shall set you free* (John 8:32).

When the Holy Spirit shines God's truth into our hearts, a transformation takes place. All darkness, gloom and despair must flee from the light of His presence. Those who are comforted have a heart that has been softened. It's a heart that is tender. It's a heart that operates from God's perspective and feels things the way God feels them because it is a heart filled with His presence. It is a heart that is repentant of the sins of the past and can recognize the consequences of these mistakes. It is a heart that continues to mourn and cry out to God saying, "Lord, change me, I don't want to be like this anymore," every time the Holy Spirit brings to light something that needs to be placed on the altar and disposed of.

It is a heart that when it comes in contact with someone else who is hurting, produces tears as it identifies with that person. What if that was me? How would I want to be treated if it were me? What does God want me to do for this person? It's a heart that begins to feel the same way God is feeling when we come into contact with sin and with its devastation and destruction around us. It is a heart that can begin to implement God's supreme strategy for victory by loving our enemies, praying for those who persecute us, and overcoming evil with good. It is a heart that understands the strategic importance of "turning the other cheek" and "going the extra mile."

There is another way to mourn. We can mourn out of bitterness because we did not get our way. We've all seen what happens when a little child doesn't get his way; he pouts and stamps and begins to cry because his will has been thwarted. That kind of mourning and those kinds of tears are not blessed. It's the other way around. That's not what God desires; He desires a heart that is set to follow Him. He wants a heart ready for Him to change, a hard heart that He has softened. He begins to soften our heart when He begins to change our heart, which is what happens when genuine conversion takes place.

Once he has plowed up the hard, fallow ground, He will plant His humility, meekness, tenderness, righteousness, and mercy in our hearts. Like an expert gardener, He will continue to cultivate His good fruit, and at the same time, pull out the weeds by the roots until our hearts are pure. His goal is to form men and women of integrity who will overcome evil with good.

Giving up our own way, and the fleeting pleasures of the world may cause us to mourn, but Jesus promises to comfort us. He will send us the Comforter, His Holy Spirit.

*Ye have heard that it was said to the ancients, Thou shalt not commit murder, and whosoever shall commit murder shall be guilty of the judgment; but I say unto you, That whosoever is angry with his brother out of control shall be in danger of the judgment, and whosoever shall insult his brother shall be in danger of the council, but whosoever shall say, Thou art impious, shall be in danger of hell.*

*Ye have heard that it was said to the ancients, Thou shalt not commit adultery; but I say unto you, That whosoever looks on a woman to lust after her has committed adultery with her already in his heart* (Matthew 5:21, 22, 27, 28).

What is Jesus describing here? He is talking about someone who is no longer thinking in the legalistic terms of the law of God, but who has been softened and is repentant from the heart. To fully understand what Jesus is telling us, we must realize that true repentance goes beyond the letter of the law.

It is not just *Thou shalt not murder*; it's not just, *Thou shalt not commit adultery*. God wants to deal with the very seeds and roots of rebellion (going our own way), wrong thoughts, and wrong feelings in our hearts before they ever get manifested into words and deeds.

*Blessed are the meek, for they shall inherit the earth.* The meek are those who submit themselves to God. *Praüs*, the Greek word translated "meek" is a very interesting word. The ancient Greeks used this word to describe their war horses, among other things. The horse was perfectly trained, ready for battle, and would go into battle and trample enemies underfoot. It would participate in the war with the rider; this was called a meek horse. The words meek and *praüs* are not identical; the translators did the best they could, but the Greek word carries a different range of meaning from ours.

I'll tell you why the Greeks called their horses *praüs*, or meek. When the horse got to the level of training where it would obey the master (the rider) no matter what was going on, it could be trusted in the heat of battle not to do something stupid or foolish. Once the rider knew that he could trust the animal, and it would obey him no matter what, he called it a meek horse even though it might be a powerful, thoroughbred stallion, capable of killing enemies in the battle.

This horse has tremendous power, capacity, and ability, but it has given up its own way and is allowing itself to be guided and ordered by the master. That is what the word *praüs* means; it means submission to the master. It doesn't mean submission to just anybody. A meek person in the biblical sense of the word is not someone who allows just anybody to tell them what to do. It is not someone who allows everyone to trample over the top of them and just goes with the flow. It is all of our gifts and abilities, everything that God has put into us, under His control and submitted to Him so that even in the worst crisis imaginable, we're not going to take the bit in our teeth and bolt on our own way. We will continue to go His way under intense pressure, persecution, danger, or need. This is what it means to be meek.

Look what happens to the meek: *Blessed are the meek, for they shall inherit the earth.* They will receive God's inheritance. They are the ones who will be placed in charge of God's creation under the Lordship of Jesus Christ, the ones who submit to Him now and allow Him to have His way in everything down to the smallest detail.

There is an interesting passage in the book of Job that people shy away from using because much of it is the advice of Job's comforters. Why would all of the philosophy and doctrine of Job's comforters, who were proven wrong in the end, be included right in the Word of God? If you look over what Job's comforters said, most of it is true. It is hard to disprove anything they said. Their only problem is that they misapplied the truth. They applied it in the wrong way at the wrong time by their human minds.

When men take God's principles and decide to apply them according to their own wisdom, they fail to provide a blessing. Job's comforters were not a blessing to Job. His crowning affliction was that he had to listen to them on top of everything else that had happened to him. But I'm not going to preach to you from words of Job's comforters. God, however, speaks out of the whirlwind in Job Chapter 39.

> *Hast thou given the horse strength? Hast thou clothed his neck with thunder? Canst thou make him leap as a grasshopper? The glory of his nostrils is formidable. He paws at the earth and rejoices in his strength; he goes forth to meet the armed men. He mocks fear and is not afraid; neither does he turn his face from the sword.*

*The quiver rattles against him, the glittering spear and the shield. He swallows the ground with fierceness and rage; the sound of the shofar does not trouble him; for the blasts of the shofar fill him with courage; he smells the battle afar off, the thunder of the princes and the sound of the battle-cry* (Job 39:19-25).

This is God's description of a "meek" horse. He lives listening for the call of that trumpet. It is his life to go charging into battle, submitted to the master who is on his back. This is what Jesus is talking about when He says: *Blessed are the meek, for they shall inherit the earth.* He's talking about people who are waiting for the sound of the trumpet blast, waiting for their orders; they can't wait to have God send them into the middle of some terrible battle in the most unexpected place. These people have no fear because they are totally submitted to Christ. When we are submitted to Him, God says that perfect love casts out fear, and He is perfect love.

There is no fear (terror) when we are in Him. Let us not confuse this with another type of fear which is the fear of the Lord – this fear is not a terror type of fear, it's a respect and a fear of being afraid of displeasing Him. If something causes you to fear such that it dominates you and modifies your behavior causing you to respond to circumstances and change your behavior to the point where you are making decisions based on fear, you are not totally submitted to Jesus Christ. You are not operating in a meek attitude of allowing Jesus Christ to be your complete Master and Lord. There may be something that you think you have submitted to God, which maybe really isn't.

Just a few months ago, when our son was two weeks old, he got very sick and was in intensive care for five days. We were not sure what was going to happen to him. There was a twinge of fear that went through my heart as we were taking our baby to the hospital. Then the thought went through my mind, "Whose baby is this? Is it mine, or is it the Lord's? Have I totally placed this child in the hands of the Lord? Am I willing for whatever God ordains for the life of this baby, my only son?"

Once I double checked that, once I reaffirmed before the Lord that this was indeed the case, the fear left. Yes, it was a difficult time, and we had to run back and forth between the hospital and home a lot. There were many different things that needed to be done. It was tiring and exhausting, but panic and fear were not there anymore.

Fear can only manipulate and control us and cause us to react when we are not totally surrendered to God. If we are willing to do what He wants, even if we lose everything or they kill us or we go through all the troubles that Job went through, Satan can't terrorize us with his fears any more.

The book of Job opens with a description of the wonderful relationship that Job had with God and of all the wonderful children, property, and possessions that God had showered upon him. From Satan's perspective, Job had everything. He complained to God that the only reason Job served God was because God had put a hedge around him and had blessed him abundantly. From God's perspective, Job lacked at least one very important thing; he still needed to learn a very important lesson. This comes out in chapter 3:

> For the thing which I greatly feared is come upon me and that which I was afraid of is come unto me. I never had prosperity, nor did I secure myself, neither was I at rest; yet trouble came (Job 3:25-26).

God's peace is not dependent on external circumstances. It is an inner state. Job had to learn to overcome his fear before he could truly become everything God wanted him to be. This is one of the reasons that God removed the hedge of protection around him, allowing Satan to strike. Even though Job was blameless in God's eyes before, during, and after his experience, God delivered him of all his fears by taking him through the middle of his worst nightmares and bringing him safely out the other side.

When I was kidnapped by the guerrillas and they threatened to kill me, the first couple of times it was, "Oh-oh, they're going to kill me!" and fear would grip me. But then in prayer before the Lord, I had to resolve: Am I willing to do and say what God wants done or said, even if they torture me, even if they shoot me? If that's the case, then they can't terrorize me anymore. It immediately takes away their weapon of fear.

When God talks of delivering us from our fears, I believe that many times the form His deliverance takes is to bring us to the place where we are willing to go forth in His name and face our worst fears because we are in submission to Jesus Christ, and this is all that matters. Then we become like the horse who doesn't like to stay in the stable.

He doesn't like to just be eating his corn or hay with an easy life in the stable. He is straining his ear for the call to battle. *He mocks fear and is not afraid; neither does he turn his face from the sword. The quiver rattles against him, the glittering spear and the shield. He swallows the ground with fierceness and rage; the sound of the shofar does not trouble him; for the blasts of the shofar fill him with courage; he smells the battle afar off, the thunder of the princes and the sound of the battle-cry* (Job 39:22-25).

He's straining his ear; he wants to find out what the commanders are saying because he's going to follow orders. He can't wait to get into the thick of it. These are the kind of people that God wants to raise up. These are the kind of people that God wants to bless. He doesn't want us to be always living in a day

When we are driving down the road, there are highway signs along the way: dangerous curve ahead, slow down – workers on the way, bridge out, speed limit. As you are going down the road, you can decide for yourself. You can say, "I'm smarter than those signs. The bridge isn't really out. I know it says slow down to 35 miles per hour, but I can still go 65." When we follow this kind of reasoning, which again has to do with our pride, we take our life into our hands, and not just our own life, but the life of anyone who might be in our car. There have been lots of terrible accidents because people did not pay attention to the signs.

As we are going along the road of life, Jesus Christ Himself, through His Holy Spirit, puts warning signs along the road. He will speak to us; He will witness to us. He'll say, "Watch it! Start putting on the brakes. You're coming into a danger zone." If we still don't watch it, He'll send someone to tell us we are skating on thin ice. He'll warn and warn and warn. If we continue to disregard all of His warnings, there comes a time when we will crash.

In the Old Testament, this is what happened to His people. Moses said,

> *I call the heavens and the earth to witness today against you that I have set before you life and death, blessing and cursing; therefore, choose life that both thou and thy seed may live, that thou may love the LORD thy God and that thou may hear his voice and that thou may cleave unto him; for he is thy life* (Deuteronomy 30:19-20).

When they went God's way, they were blessed, and when they went their own way, they found danger and difficulties that ended with their beautiful city of Jerusalem being destroyed two times (Deuteronomy 30:15-20).

God is the same yesterday, today and forever. But now,

through the death and resurrection of our Lord Jesus Christ, we can have His presence inside of us. We (in the church age) have a greater opportunity to live according to God's will than anyone who has gone before us in human history. We have the opportunity to recall those who have gone before us and learn from their mistakes. In Colombia, they have taken cars that are smashed in on all sides and set them up in some of the key intersections to remind people by saying, "See what happened to those people. We don't want that to happen to us."

Some of the greatest men of God made some horrible slip-ups and lost important blessings. King David was a man after God's own heart, but because of his sin of adultery and murder, the Lord declared that bloodshed would never leave his family; he would experience problems with violence in his family in the future even though he was personally restored. David went through that terrible problem with his son, Absalom. God has allowed these examples to be recorded so we won't have to experience similar things; we can learn from what happened to other people. If we are willing to be poor in spirit, let God deal with our pride, and mourn our own deeds and our own way, God will send us the Holy Spirit that we might submit ourselves totally to Jesus Christ. If we choose His way, God says the kingdom of the heavens is ours, and we will inherit the earth.

*Blessed are those who hunger and thirst for righteousness, for they shall be satisfied.* The new birth, birth into the realm of the Spirit, will produce hunger and thirst for righteousness (being filled with the character of God), just like natural babies hunger and thirst for milk. The motivation of the heart changes, and our new nature now hungers and thirsts for righteousness (being and doing what God wants). We must feed our new nature daily by allowing the Holy Spirit to have His way in our lives. This is the requirement for continually being filled to overflowing (baptized) with the presence of God's Spirit. Those who attempt to live solely on their past experiences with God will stagnate.

In many churches people are introduced to the "baptism" of the Holy Spirit by repeating funny phrases after the teacher. They are told to talk baby talk and just open their mouth and say any strange phrase that pops into their mind. That's not what the "baptism" is at all. We must allow God to deal with our pride until we mourn the deeds of the old man under the old nature. Those who mourn will be comforted with the genuine Holy Spirit. There must be a genuine seeking after God. We must allow God to break the hardness of our heart. When He changes our heart and gives us His heart, it comes with that hunger and thirst for righteousness and for meekly doing things His way. The person who receives the genuine infilling of the presence of God need not strive after superficial manifestations of spirituality; this person simply begins to bubble over, to overflow with the supernatural presence and love of God. Jesus promises a well of "living water" that will spring up out of our innermost being (John 7:38).

There are counterfeit spiritual experiences in the world. Many try to bypass the only true entrance to the kingdom of God. They refuse to enter at the narrow gate. They refuse to allow God to deal with their pride. They refuse to give up their own way. They want prosperity and blessing, but they refuse to embrace the cross of Christ. These are those who falsely think they have been saved when in reality they are not, those who falsely think that they've been filled with the Holy Spirit when they are not. They've been filled with some other spirit, some cheap spirit that will neither produce nor satisfy a genuine hunger and thirst for righteousness.

Whole groups of "Christian" people are just playing games with one another. The tragic thing is that the fruit isn't there. The battle isn't being won. Their house is built on the sand, and when the storm comes, everything they have placed their trust in will come down with a great crash (Matthew 7:27).

There are large sectors of Christendom where instead of a witness being given for the Lord, the overall testimony has been against the Lord. Lofty ministries have come crashing to the ground. The end result in the eyes of the world has been to give the Lord a black eye. The salt has lost its savor and has been trampled underfoot (Matthew 5:13).

God wants to change this. He wants to give us the victory. He wants us to charge into the battle like the horse described in Job Chapter 39. He doesn't want us bound by our fears living in a cage that we have made for ourselves. He doesn't want Satan to hem us in. He wants us to go forth into victory without any fear in our hearts. God says, "He (the meek horse) laughs at fear and strains his ear for the trumpet, for the sound of the commander and the battle cry." He can't wait to engage the enemy.

> *For the idols have spoken vanity and the diviners have seen a lie and have told vain dreams; they comfort in vain; therefore they went their way like sheep; they were humbled because there was no shepherd.*
>
> *My anger is kindled against the pastors, and I will visit the he goats, for the LORD of the hosts shall visit his flock, the house of Judah, and shall make them as his horse of honour in the battle. Out of him shall come the corner, out of him the stake, out of him the battle bow, out of him also every oppressor.*
>
> *And they shall be as mighty men, who tread down their enemies in the mire of the streets in the battle; and they shall fight because the LORD shall be with them, and the riders on horses shall be confounded* (Zechariah 10:2-5).

In Old Testament typology, the horse represents man's effort or strength. Thus, those who do battle on horseback, trusting in horses instead of the Lord, are put to shame. On the other hand, God promises to make those who submit their gifts, abilities, and strength to Him into His own (corporate) royal horse that He Himself will ride to battle and win the victory.

*And I saw the heaven open, and behold a white horse; and he that was seated upon him was called Faithful and True, and in righteousness he judges and makes war* (Revelation 19:11).

LET US PRAY:

*Heavenly Father, we want to be Your royal horse in battle. We want to be meek before you. We want to be like Moses who was willing to listen to you and who was patient with the people around him. He did not assert his own authority, but allowed you to establish his authority as a leader, truly called by Yourself. Lord, we want to win a victory, but first of all Lord, we want to be sure our hearts are as You desire them to be.*

*Lord, if there is a hard spot in our hearts, we want You to break it up. We want You to come in and plough up the fallow ground. We want You to soften our hearts; to tenderize our hearts. We want You to give us Your heart. Lord, we want to feel the way that You do about the things that are wrong in our lives. We want to feel the way that You do about our gifts and our abilities and all the wonderful things that You have blessed us with. We want to be able to manage these things for You, and for this we need to have Your presence within us.*

*Lord, we want to examine our hearts before You. Search us, oh God, and if there be any wicked way within us, please cleanse us, Lord. Clean us up. If we are dominated by fear, please help us that we might surrender those areas to You. We ask You to conquer our fear with Your love, that we might go forward with you to the battle, straining our ears for the trumpet sound for our orders. May our thoughts and feelings not be: Oh no, what if God asks me to do something I don't want to do? What if God were to ask me to go across the world and be a missionary in a country where I don't want to go? What if God were to ask me to give up my job or to give up my car, or my home? May we not be bound and paralyzed by fear.*

*Lord, we ask You to change our hearts so our thoughts and our feelings might be totally different and we might be straining, trying to catch the sound of the commanders and the battle cry, straining for the sound of the trumpet from afar. "Could that trumpet call be for me? Could there be a battle that God wants me to engage in some place? How can I get there? How soon can I get there?" May we move on to wherever the action is, to wherever the battle is, straining to hear our orders, ready at any moment, looking to You, Lord Jesus, for even the smallest things like the horse submits to the details and rigors of training so it can face the real battle when it comes.*

*Lord, help us to look at every little detail as something important that we need to be faithful to You in, so we might not be mediocre Christians, but that we might excel in executing whatever orders You might give us with whatever tiny responsibility You might want us to be faithful in, so You might give us more important things as we mature. May the day come when we can face all of the attacks, even the most powerful attacks that the enemy can mount, and we can look the worst demon in the eye and not feel any fear, but just be listening attentively for Your orders as to what to do and how to put the enemy under our feet. Change our thinking, Lord, change our hearts. Let us think Your thoughts, let us feel Your feelings. Let us go forth in joy and victory to serve You.*

*Amen.*

Chapter Three

The war horse in the last chapter was trained for battle, snorting, stamping and straining to hear the sound of the trumpet and the shout of the commanders. This horse is described by the Greek word, *praüs*, or meek, because the horse is perfectly trained, perfectly submitted to its master, and can be relied upon to obey orders even in the heat and confusion of battle. I would like to give you another example of meekness:

> *Now the man Moses was very meek, above all the men which were upon the face of the earth* (Numbers 12:3).

Moses started his career by taking the law into his own hands and killing an Egyptian. Moses was a killer before God dealt with him out in the desert, preparing and training him to do battle God's way. Moses submitted to God and became meek. God then used Moses beyond the maximum potential that he could think of.

Maybe Moses stuttered; he didn't think that he could speak on God's behalf. Yet God brought Moses to face Pharaoh, who was the most dangerous figure of the day. Pharaoh had enslaved God's people and ordered the killing of innocent children. God sent Moses to confront Pharaoh, backing him up with one of the most awesome displays of power that has ever occurred in human history. The ten plagues ended in God breaking the back of Pharaoh and his army, destroying them in the Red Sea and giving freedom to His people.

If we submit to God and allow Him to have His way in and through us, we will see amazing events take place. God will begin to utilize us above and beyond what we consider our potential to be. Each of us has been created by God with special gifts and abilities; none of us are the same. We will never be truly happy and satisfied until we utilize our God-given gifts and abilities to their maximum potential. And we won't be able to utilize what we have to our maximum potential unless we are surrendered to Jesus Christ, unless we are meek, unless He's the Master and we are submitted to Him, willing to do things His way. When God chose to interrupt the downward moral slide of human history by direct revelation of His will (law) to mankind, He chose the meekest man on earth (Moses) as a channel for His power.

I was speaking to a group of young people, and I shared the experience of when I shot my foot with a .22-caliber rifle at age fifteen. On the one hand, I had been asking the Lord to intervene in my life and help me get my schoolwork done on time. (I was studying high school by correspondence and had trouble managing my time.) On the other hand, I continued to goof off and do anything except what I was supposed to be doing. As I fell further and further behind schedule (I couldn't seem to bring myself to hit the books), I continued to plead with the Lord for help. I told the Lord that He could have a free hand to do anything He wanted in my life if He would only help me to get through high school on time. Finally, one evening I had a hunting accident (while I was goofing off) and shot myself in the foot. This laid me up in the hospital for quite a while (Infection had set in and several doctors even suggested cutting my foot off). I ended up developing good study habits. When I studied hard, my foot got better, and when I goofed off, it got worse. I finished my course on time and also scored very high on my college entrance exams.

One girl came up to me after my talk and said, "I'm never

going to commit my life totally to the Lord like you did. What if something like that were to happen to me."

Afterwards I thought, "What if God had not intervened in my life? What if He had not disciplined me every time that I needed it? Where would I be today? I would be a mediocre Christian, doing mediocre things, incapable of facing the enemy, incapable of winning a victory, wandering around in the wilderness of my own good intentions, wallowing in prosperity, useless for participating in the army of God."

It was God's mercy and God's love for me that allowed Him at several key times in my life to make me very uncomfortable, to prick the bubble of my pride, my will, and my own way to the point where I was willing to bow to Him and say, "Okay Lord, You can have it Your way. My ideas aren't as good as I thought they were. I want Your better ideas, I want Your best way."

Without real Christians, without a living demonstration of the presence of Jesus Christ living within us, it is not possible to evangelize effectively. The Bible says that unless the Father draws men, they cannot come to Jesus Christ (John 6:44). How is the Father going to draw them to Christ if we represent Christ, and people look at us and cannot see Christ in us? How is this supposed to happen? (Matthew 5:14).

God says that He wants to write His laws on the tablets of our hearts so we will not be under a legalistic law of do's and don'ts. By His grace (power), He can change our hearts and motivate us from within. He wants to place His Spirit within us and sensitize our consciences so that whenever we are in a difficult situation, we will automatically be prompted to respond in the manner that God wants.

Let's look at the Ten Commandments in Deuteronomy Chapter 5.

*And Moses called all Israel and said unto them, Hear,*

*O Israel, the statutes and rights which I speak in your
ears this day, that ye may learn them and keep them,
to do them. The LORD our God made a covenant with
us in Horeb. Not with our fathers did the LORD make
this covenant, but with us, all of us who are here alive
this day.*

*The LORD spoke with you face to face in the mount out
of the midst of the fire (I stood between the LORD and
you at that time, to show you the word of the LORD,
for ye were afraid by reason of the fire and did not
climb the mount)...* (Deuteronomy 5:1-5).

Only one man went up to the mountain to receive God's
law, and that man was Moses. This man has been given as an
example of meekness. He was the only one who was unafraid
of the fire of the presence of God. He went up the mountain
while the trumpet blast and the thunder and the lightning of
the presence of God caused the rest of the children of Israel to
cower in fear.

When it is time to hear from God, what is our reaction? Is
it fear? "No, no, no! Not me. I'm not going to have anything to
do with the trumpet and with the fire and with the thunder
and with the lightning. I don't want to speak face to face with
God. I can't stand to listen to God. What if He were to tell me
to do something that I don't want to do? What if He were to
want me to give up something that I don't want to give up?"

That's the way the children of Israel were. Things have not
changed much with the Christian church either. Most people
would rather be comfortable and have somebody else go hear
from God instead; maybe their pastor, or their priest, can go
hear from God. We'll listen to him when he comes back. But
we don't really want to hear from God ourselves; we don't really

ally felt that this meant swearing. But it isn't just swearing. It's saying, "Thus saith the Lord..." when the Lord did not say it. It's saying, "Hallelujah, praise the Lord," when we are not being obedient to the Lord. It's coming in and singing all the songs and saying we are in agreement with the Christian faith, identifying ourselves as the people of God, when we are not living our life in obedience to the Lord.

Imagine a business manager of a large corporation who has control of the company check book. He is supposed to write checks to finance the needs and objectives of the company. What would happen to him if he started writing unauthorized company checks for a new house, a new car, a brand new swimming pool, and anything else he felt like for his own personal use? Someone like this would be put in jail in very short order. When the Lord promises that whatsoever we ask for in His name, He is going to do, it is not a magical formula. Some people think we can ask for anything we want and just tack, "in Jesus' name," on the end of our prayer, and it's supposed to happen.

When we use the name of the Lord, it means that our petition is on behalf of the Lord. In other words, when He has called us and given us our orders, we are in His will; then, when we ask according to His will, He will provide what we need to stay in His will and get His job done. That is what He is saying. We cannot take promises that apply to His will and use them for personal gain, any more than a business manager can take the corporate funds and pocket them for whatever He pleases.

The Christian church is full of people asking for everything under the sun in Jesus' name when really it is in their own name. Some of us have a gift and anointing of persuading others of truth, the ability to be preachers, teachers, evangelists, or to minister through music. If we take our God-given gifts and start using them for our own benefit, we are taking the anointing of God and pouring it over our own heads. We will short circuit the blessing of the Lord and will be guilty of taking the name of the Lord in vain.

If we are just trying to stamp the Lord's name all over the top of our own selfish plans and ambitions (individual or corporate) to dress them up and make them look nice and acceptable, we are taking the Lord's name in vain. We may not have any literal idols, but if we are spending our time and money on good things that keep us from pursuing God's best, these things become our idols.

God wants to write His laws on the tablets of our hearts. God wants to write the essence of the Ten Commandments that the Jews could not keep on the tablets of our hearts. He wants to change our hearts. He wants to give us His feelings. He wants to motivate us from within to hunger and thirst for His righteousness, so He can fill and satisfy us. He wants to fill us with Himself. When we are full of the Lord and begin to get a little inkling of how God feels about sin, it has a tremendous impact on our behavior.

The first three commandments deal with our relationship with God. The next seven commandments concern man's relationship to man. If our relationship with God is not right, we will not be able to maintain a satisfactory relationship with one another either.

When we are submitted to the Lord and in a proper relationship with Him, He says, *My yoke is easy and my burden is light.* The children of Israel thought that if they went up on that mountain to hear the Word of the Lord, everything they held dear would be burned up in God's fire; they might lose their very lives; they could not come into the presence of God and live. This is what Satan will try to tell us. He will try to tell us that unless we hang onto the things that we hold dear, we won't be happy. This is not true. The only way to be happy is to die to our own selfish way and surrender everything to

Jesus Christ. The happiest people I know are the ones who don't have many physical possessions, the ones who live for others and for the Lord.

> *Honour thy father and thy mother, as the LORD thy God has commanded thee; that thy days may be prolonged and that it may go well with thee, in the land which the LORD thy God gives thee.*
>
> *Thou shalt not murder.*
>
> *Thou shalt not commit adultery.*
>
> *Thou shalt not steal.*
>
> *Thou shalt not give false testimony against thy neighbor.*
>
> *Thou shalt not desire thy neighbour's wife, neither shalt thou covet thy neighbour's house, his field or his manservant or his maidservant, his ox or his ass or any thing that is thy neighbour's* (Deuteronomy 5:16-21).

In the Sermon on the Mount, Jesus takes the Ten Commandments to a new level:

> *Ye have heard that it was said to the ancients, Thou shalt not commit murder, and whosoever shall commit murder shall be guilty of the judgment;*
>
> *but I say unto you, That whosoever is angry with his brother out of control shall be in danger of the judgment, and whosoever shall insult his brother shall be in danger of the council, but whosoever shall say, Thou art impious, shall be in danger of hell* (Matthew 5:21-22).

Here Jesus applies the law to the inward state of our hearts. Hatred towards our brother is the moral equivalent of murder under the New Covenant. Lust is the same as adultery. Jesus tells us that the status of our hearts will determine our outward conduct (Matthew 15:18-20).

Look what Moses says at the end of the Ten Commandments:

> These words the LORD spoke unto all your congregation in the mount out of the midst of the fire, of the cloud, and of the thick darkness, with a great voice, and he added no more. And he wrote them in two tables of stone and delivered them unto me. And it came to pass when ye heard the voice out of the midst of the darkness and saw the mountain that burned with fire that ye came near unto me, even all the princes of your tribes and your elders; and ye said, Behold, the LORD our God has shown us his glory and his greatness, and we have heard his voice out of the midst of the fire; we have seen this day that God does talk with man, and he lives.
>
> Now, therefore, why should we die? For this great fire will consume us; if we hear the voice of the LORD our God any more, then we shall die.
>
> For what is all flesh that it should hear the voice of the living God that speaks out of the midst of the fire, as we heard, and live?
>
> Go thou near and hear all that the LORD our God shall say, and thou shalt tell us all that the LORD our God shall speak unto thee; and we will hear it, and do it (Deuteronomy 5:22-27).

Some said, and still today say, "Okay, God spoke. Yes, the Bible is inspired. I believe it. But I'm going to continue to make my own plans. I'm going to continue to make up my own good ideas. Whenever the pastor has something he feels is a real revelation from God, he can share it on Sunday morning, and I'll listen. But I'm afraid of that intimate communion, that intimate contact with God, because the things that I hold dear (my own way) might get burned up in the fire."

Let me tell you what happened to the generation that went out with this attitude after such a tremendous revelation from God. Guess what happened to them? They all died in the wilderness. None of them made it into the Promised Land. A new generation was raised up under Joshua and Caleb that went into the Promised Land. The mentality of being slaves that they had brought from Egypt, the fleshly mentality of depending on worldly comforts, the cage they brought with them, they were never able to totally overcome. Even though God delivered them physically out of the land of Egypt with an awesome display of His power and might, He was unable to get the Egypt out of most of them, and they wandered around in the wilderness until the entire generation (except two men) died.

God does not want this to happen to us. In the New Testament, it specifically says that these things are recorded so we can learn from them (Jude 5), and they won't happen to us. God wants to speak to us. He wants His living Word to be within our hearts. He wants to have full authority over our lives. He wants to be able to discipline us when we need it. He wants to be able to bless us, to prosper us, to open and close doors for us. He wants to be able to use us effectively, but He cannot do this as long as we cling to something for ourselves instead of onto Him.

If we really want to walk a life of victory and be used of God effectively, there is no other way, but to put everything on the altar. There is no other way, but to say, "Lord, there are aspects of my life that I might not even be aware of, but I want You to deal with anything that needs to be dealt with. Even if there is an area in my life where I'm not willing or capable of making the proper commitment, make me willing. You are God. You are sovereign. You can do anything."

But God has chosen to limit Himself in one little area in His relationship with man. He is a gentleman. He has manners. He is not rude or obnoxious. He does not impose Himself on people who do not want Him around. If you want your relationship with God to be aloof, He will respect your will. He won't force Himself on you. But He also says, *Draw nigh unto Me, and I will draw nigh unto you,* and *Blessed are the meek, for they shall inherit the earth.* They will be fulfilled and satisfied above and beyond their wildest dreams. Nothing satisfies more than obeying God.

Prior to the time when I was kidnapped, I did not have much to show for being a missionary, maybe a handful of people that I had influenced for God. But since that time, the Lord has given me the joy of being able to work with a large number of people and has allowed me to have the satisfaction of seeing many of them grow more like the Lord Jesus Christ. This is real satisfaction. It is lasting satisfaction. The godly character that is developed in us or in others will be ours to enjoy for all eternity.

*Blessed are those who hunger and thirst for righteousness, for they will be filled.* Do you hunger and thirst for righteousness? Or is righteousness something that is optional? Is righteousness for you like dessert; you can take it or leave it? Or do you have to have it? Is it something you can't live without? Remember, righteousness means both doing what God desires and being what God designed us to be. In Spanish, Greek, and Hebrew, the words for righteousness and justice are the same word. God wants us to hunger and thirst for what is right, what He approves of, and what He promises to fill us with.

Don't settle for second best. Don't settle for a superficial experience with the Lord. Don't settle for hearing from somebody else who's heard from the Lord. Don't let anybody else get between you and God. Don't live on borrowed revelation. Don't shy away from the fire. Don't be like many in America today; they want to be filled with the Holy Spirit, speak in tongues, and have emotional experiences, but they don't want the fire because the fire might burn something up they hold dear. John the Baptist said:

> *I indeed baptize you in water unto repentance, but he that comes after me is mightier than I, whose shoes I am not worthy to bear; he shall baptize you in the Holy Spirit and fire, whose fan is in his hand; and he will thoroughly purge his threshing floor and gather his wheat into the storehouse, but he will burn up the chaff with fire that shall never be quenched* (Matthew 3:11-12).

We have taken the message of John the Baptist on repentance and cut it in half. We have decided to let God be the God of what's wrong. He can tell us what's wrong; if we have broken any of His commandments, then we will repent, but we still want to decide what is right. We refuse to expose our good plans and our good desires to his fire to see if there is any chaff. We are still clinging to a piece of the fruit of the tree of the knowledge of good and evil; and that half of the apple that we refuse to give up (the knowledge of choosing what is good for ourselves) is still blocking our access to the tree of life (the full blessing, power and glory of the risen Christ).

When it comes to the Holy Spirit, some only want the fun things. They want the emotional experiences. They want to impress others with their spirituality. They want the baptism of the Holy Spirit, but they don't want the fire. So, they take half of what the Bible teaches on repentance and half of what Jesus offers us. They want His Spirit, but they don't want His fire, and then they wonder why Satan is overcoming the church, why we can't stand against temptation, why so much evil is going on around us, why the harvest isn't coming, and why our children or our parents aren't what we think they ought to be. The answer: we aren't what we ought to be. We need to return to the way the Lord Jesus Christ taught. We need to repent of our own way and our good ideas along with the things that we know to be wrong.

The church has lost God's fire. The fire is not there like it was before. We must get back to the fire; we must go back up that mountain and hear from God. We need to plunge right into the middle of the fire and lightning that the children of Israel wanted to shy away from. "Oh, no, we don't want to hear any more from God. We don't want to be near that fire lest we die."

This is what it is all about: to be effective for God, we must die. We must participate in the death and resurrection of Jesus Christ. We must die to our own way where we are controlled by our corrupt natural desires. Our natural desires must be nailed to the cross with Jesus Christ so the power of His resurrection life might spring forth inside of us and manifest the power of His grace to a world that is lost and dying.

This is the gospel of the kingdom according to Jesus Christ, not according to anybody else. This is the gospel that Jesus Christ Himself proclaimed in the Beatitudes. He taught first of all about those who are poor in spirit, the ones who have chosen to let go of their pride. Genuine repentance is the only way into the kingdom of heaven. Those who mourn with a contrite heart will be comforted. God will send the Comforter to lift them up and restore their faith. Only the genuine presence of the Holy Spirit in our lives can cause us to be meek. The meek, those who totally submit to the Master, are the only ones who will inherit the earth. They are on the winning team. They will overcome the enemy.

When the Holy Spirit comes in, what does He do? He breaks the power of the flesh (circumcises our hearts) and writes the laws of God on the tablets of our hearts. We begin to respond to situations the way that God would want us to respond, in meekness and out of a restored sense of His justice, mercy, and faithfulness.

When repentance (turning from going our own way) and faith (submission to and confidence in God so we might go His way) start producing a change in our hearts, God starts giving us the desires of His heart; we start hungering and thirsting for His righteousness because this is what God yearns for in us. He will give us that same longing, that same hunger and thirst for doing and being right. He promises to fulfill and satisfy us.

*Blessed are the merciful, for they shall obtain mercy.*

Mercy is more than superficially forgiving others. Mercy is treating other people the way we would want God to treat us if we were in the other person's shoes. Have you ever wondered how to treat someone else? I believe that any true Christian can instinctively know how God wants us to respond to others around us no matter how difficult the situation. God says we are to love our neighbors as ourselves. What if I was causing an awful problem? How would I want to be treated? How would I want to be corrected if I needed correction? How would I want God to treat me if I were in the position of that other person? We all know how we would desire to be treated, so all we need to do is put ourselves in the other fellow's position, and God will reveal a course of action that is both just and merciful.

Mercy is not letting other people get away with murder. Sometimes the most merciful thing we can do with one of our children is some very sharp correction. But unless that correction comes from a loving heart and unless a loving relationship has been established between us, our attempt at discipline may fail because the child will not have the proper respect for our authority. Instead of correcting the situation, our unmerciful application of justice will backfire, and our children will become bitter. For this reason, the Bible says that the fathers are not to provoke their children to wrath.

*Blessed are the merciful for they shall obtain mercy.* This really means planting mercy. It means treating other people the way that we would like to have God treat us. The Bible says we reap what we sow. If we are asking God for things and want Him to solve problems in our lives, we cannot turn our backs on someone who comes to us with a problem that we can solve and then continue, "Oh Lord, please help me." How do you think the Lord will feel about us? Is He going to want to help us? Will He feel like helping someone who is ungrateful? Will He continue to bless someone who partakes of His blessing and mercy, but refuses to share it with anyone else? Many times God continues to help us when we do not deserve it, but there is a limit to His patience.

Another aspect of this involves forgiveness. Humanly speaking, we can forgive someone who comes to us in repentance and says, "Oh, I'll never do it again. Please forgive me. I'm so sorry. I'll make it right."

It is within our human capabilities to say, "All right, buster, you better not do it again. I'll forgive you just this once. I won't forget it, but I'll forgive you." But what about someone who has hurt us, is continuing to hurt us, and will probably keep on hurting us in the future? How about forgiving someone like that? In the natural, it is impossible. Jesus was the only one who could hang on the cross and say, *Father, forgive them. They don't know what they are doing.*

If we are to forgive others from the heart, we need the kind of mercy that only He can place within our hearts. If we allow Him to plant his forgiveness and mercy in our lives, they will have a cleansing, purifying effect on our hearts. But we need to remember one very important thing – our desire to forgive others must be manifested in merciful words and deeds towards those who have wronged us in order for God's dynamic of blessing to be fulfilled in our lives and extended through us to those around us. This is how to overcome our enemies God's way.

*Blessed are the pure in heart, for they shall see God.* Have you ever been confused and unable to see God? You don't know where God is, you don't know why so many difficult things are happening to you. You're confused; everything seems to be coming down around you. Where is God? If you cannot see God in your life in spite of the difficult circumstances you may be going through, check your heart. It might be that your heart is not pure before God. It might be that there is a root of bitterness, a little unforgiveness, or a lack of mercy in your heart. Even if you have been an innocent victim of the slights, selfishness, and abuse of those around you, you can still be emotionally scarred by what has happened if you refuse to forgive those who have hurt you. Then you will lose sight of God.

Our hearts are mirrors of our souls. Our hearts are designed to reflect God. If that mirror is dirty, it will not reflect a clear image of God. Not only will we not see God, nobody else will see God reflected in us either. Do others see the image of Jesus Christ in you? Or is the image of Christ that they see in you a distorted image, coming out of a dirty or warped mirror that distorts a beautiful and loving God, making Him look grotesque? If our hearts are pure, they will reflect God. The Bible says we are created in the image of God. This is how we were created, and then we fell. God wants to restore His image to perfection inside each one of us by purifying our hearts. He wants us to respond to the injury and injustice in the world around us by reflecting His image. We are to overcome evil with good.

*Be ye therefore perfect, even as your Father who is in the heavens is perfect* (Matthew 5:48).

With our human limitations, it is hard, if not impossible, to be perfect. So why is God asking us this of us? Because there is one area in our lives that can be perfect and that is our heart (our will and motivation). God wants to take our heart out, the heart of stone, and replace it with a heart of flesh, His heart; and His heart is perfect. If we want, we can have a pure heart. We can have His heart. We can be included in the body of Jesus Christ. His heart is big enough to include all of us.

If there are others that you have excluded from your heart, others that you have kicked out of your heart, remember that it is impossible to hate your brother and love God at the same time (1 John 4:20). If you want Jesus to prevail in your heart, you have to open your heart to everyone. You have to be willing to have a place in your heart for your worst enemy, and the Lord will make that place because it is His heart. If you want to know how to relate to those around you, it is very simple; just have a place for them in your heart. Deal with them from the heart, and the Lord will show you what to do.

Think for a few minutes on the status of your heart. Can you see God? Or is your image of God fuzzy? Do things happen, and you say, "I have trouble getting a word from the Lord? I have trouble hearing the voice of the Lord. It's not crystal clear like it used to be, or like it ought to be."

If you are not hearing the voice of the Lord clearly, there is some major surgery that needs to be done in your heart. God is not in the business of trying to polish and renew your old stone heart. He wants to do a heart transplant; He wants to give you His heart. He wants to restore His image in us. Let Him do it. Tell Him that He is free to work in your heart. Tell Him that He is free to cleanse your heart, to remove any trace of unforgiveness or bitterness.

LET US PRAY:

*Heavenly Father, help us to repent. We can't even repent properly on our own. We need Your help to turn from our own way. We need Your help to see that our good ideas are not as good as we think they are. We need Your help to be able to submit our good ideas unto You and allow You to change them as necessary. Lord, we don't want a superficial, emotional experience. Lord, we want the real thing. We want what John the Baptist promised. We want the Holy Spirit and fire.*

*Send us your fire, Lord, and take away our fear. Purge our hearts of all that is not right; circumcise our hearts so we might please you and become the temple of your Holy Spirit. Write your commandments on the tablets of our hearts and in our minds. Show us your ways that we might walk in them. Fill us with Your love and Your anointing so we will have Your goals and use Your gifts properly, not to try to obtain things for ourselves, but to build Your kingdom and edify Your body. In this day and age when much of Your house is in ruins, Lord, may we be part of Your restoration. May we be living stones in Your temple not made of hands. May we deny ourselves and live for You.*
*Amen.*

## Chapter Four

I was speaking in a penitentiary to a group of prisoners, and I had just finished explaining Matthew 5:21-23 about how the feelings of bitterness and anger in our hearts are equated by the Lord with murder and how when we begin to put other people down, condemning the motives of their hearts, our relationship with them is broken. One of the inmates came up afterwards and said to me, "You're right on, brother. That was a true word. That's the way it is." I conversed with him more, and he said, "Yup, that's what happened to me. I started feeling anger against my brother and my father. I started insulting them and questioning their motives. Then one day I picked up a gun and shot both of them, and that's why I'm here."

In a split second of bitterness, rage, and anger, he had killed his brother and his father, and now he was spending his life in prison. That blew me away. I didn't know what to say. We can look at a shocking case like this with horror, but when we begin to assassinate someone's character and kick them out of our heart, God looks at it as if we had just finished murdering our brother.

The sixth beatitude is *Blessed are the pure in heart, for they shall see God.* If I could sum up "the pure in heart" in one word, the word I would choose would be integrity. This is very close to the meaning of the Hebrew word *shalom* or peace which means "wholesomeness" and is derived from a root which means "to be safe." Integrity is the key to obtaining God's blessing; this is what He wants to form in us. He wants us to be men and women of integrity. Of all the verses of the Sermon on the Mount (there are 111 of them), more than half are devoted to the issue of hypocrisy vs. integrity.

The greatest danger to those of us in the Christian church after we have come into a knowledge of His saving grace is the possibility of falling into hypocrisy. You remember there was a case among the apostles of the early church. Paul admonished Peter publicly for doing and saying things in one way privately, but in another way publicly. He accepted the Gentile believers privately, but when the Jews were present, he did not want to have anything to do with them.

> And the other Jews dissembled likewise with him, (Peter) insomuch that Barnabas also was carried away with their hypocrisy.
>
> But when I saw that they did not walk uprightly according to the truth of the gospel, I said unto Peter before them all, If thou, being a Jew, dost live after the manner of Gentiles, and not as do the Jews, why dost thou compel the Gentiles to live as do the Jews? (Galatians 2:13-14).

This happened between Peter, Barnabas, and Paul. How much more danger to each and every one of us? Fortunately, for the work of the Lord in the early church, this conflict was resolved. Peter became convinced of the truth that Paul was proclaiming and not only changed his conduct, but threw his complete support behind the ministry and epistles of Paul as evidenced in Scriptures such as Acts Chapter 15 and 2 Peter 3:15.

Let's look at what the Lord has to say. Hypocrisy is the exact opposite of integrity. Matthew 6 starts out like this:

> Take heed not to do your alms (acts of mercy) before men, to be seen of them; otherwise, ye have no reward of your Father who is in the heavens. Therefore, when thou doest thine alms, do not sound a trumpet before thee,

*as the hypocrites do in the synagogues and in the streets that they may have glory of men. Verily I say unto you, They already have their reward. But when thou doest alms, let not thy left hand know what thy right hand doeth that thine alms may be in secret; and thy Father who sees in secret, he shall reward thee openly.*

*And when thou prayest, thou shalt not be as the hypocrites are, for they love to pray standing in the synagogues and in the corners of the streets that they may be seen of men. Verily I say unto you, They already have their reward. But thou, when thou prayest, enter into thy chamber, and when thou hast shut thy door, pray to thy Father who is in secret; and thy Father who sees in secret shall reward thee openly.*

*But when ye pray, use not vain repetitions as the worldly do, for they think that they shall be heard for their much speaking* (Matthew 6:1-7).

Then it goes on to give us what we call the Lord's prayer, which perhaps could also be called the disciples' prayer because He wants every true disciple to pray according to these guidelines. It is a prayer exalting God and asking for God's will to be done. If we correlate the seven premises of the Lord's Prayer with the Beatitudes, they line up perfectly (we will look at this in chapter ten). If we have received Jesus' message (The Beatitudes), this is the response He is waiting for from our hearts:

*Ye, therefore, are to pray like this: Our Father who art in the heavens, Hallowed be thy name. Thy kingdom come. Thy will be done in earth, as it is in heaven. Give us this day our daily bread. And set us free from our debts, as we set free our debtors. And lead us not into*

*temptation, but deliver us from evil, for thine is the
kingdom and the power and the glory forever. Amen.*

*For if ye set men free from their trespasses, your heav-
enly Father will also set you free; but if ye do not set
men free from their trespasses, neither will your Father
set you free from your trespasses."* (Matthew 6:9-15).

The Lord's Prayer is given right in the middle of Jesus' teaching against hypocrisy. It is tragic that many hypocrites are in the
habit of repeating the Lord's Prayer without taking it to heart.

*Moreover when ye fast, be not as the hypocrites, of a
sad countenance, for they disfigure their faces that they
may appear unto men to fast. Verily I say unto you.
They already have their reward. But thou, when thou
dost fast, anoint thine head, and wash thy face that
thou appear not unto men to fast, but unto thy Father
who is in secret; and thy Father, who sees in secret,
shall reward thee openly* (Matt. 6:16-18).

The Lord's pattern in the Sermon on the Mount is: don't be
like that, be like this. Don't do it the way the world teaches, do
it My way. Don't live according to the world's standards, live
according to My standards. Be the kind of people that I want
you to be.

Unfortunately for evangelical Christianity, many times the
emphasis has been on believing dogma with our minds. Undue
emphasis in believing doctrinal statements (other than the written Word of God) will put a rift between us and other parts of
the body of Christ if we happen to (in good faith) believe dif-
ferently. Each little group has different beliefs, and these beliefs
are zealously fought over.

Not that there is anything inherently wrong with having
our beliefs straight in our heads, but this is not the center of
importance. The center of Christianity is that we become the

people God wants us to be so we can faithfully do the work He has called us to do. Christ must dominate the very center of our being. Until we allow the Lord to do a work in our hearts, it is not easy to get our minds straightened out. God wants to work on our hearts first. He wants to put His attitudes, His feelings, His heart within us. Then working from there, He can begin to build the logical aspects of dogma and doctrine in our minds. Because both Paul and Peter had the same Spirit in their hearts, they were able to straighten out their doctrinal conflicts.

*Lay not up for yourselves treasures upon the earth, where moth and rust corrupt, and where thieves break through and steal; but lay up for yourselves treasures in heaven, where neither moth nor rust corrupt and where thieves do not break through nor steal; for where your treasure is, there will your heart be also* (Matthew 6:19-21).

Notice that Jesus does not say where your treasure is, there your mind will be also. Jesus says that where your treasure is, there will your heart be also. The Sermon on the Mount focuses on the attitudes of our hearts, on where our heart is. He goes on to say:

*The lamp of the body is the eye: if therefore thine eye is sincere, thy whole body shall be full of light. But if thine eye is evil, thy whole body shall be full of darkness. If, therefore, the light that is in thee is darkness, how great is that darkness! No one can serve two masters, for either he will hate the one and love the other or else he will hold to the one and despise the other. Ye cannot serve God and riches* (Matthew 6:22-24).

You cannot serve both God and the things of this world. You cannot want to have a good time here and get all the things the world has to offer and still be devoted to God. You must make a decision. Either you are going to decide for what God wants, meaning you will take up your cross, follow the Lord and make sacrifices whenever He asks you to make them, or you will go after the things of this world and lose the real treasures which are in heaven. No one can serve two masters.

One of the main problems I have seen in the church is that there are a lot people trying to serve two masters. In the book of Ezekiel, God explains to the prophet why he destroyed His temple in Jerusalem.

> *And he said unto me, Son of man, this is the place of my throne, and the place of the soles of my feet, in which I will dwell in the midst of the sons of Israel for ever, and my holy name, the house of Israel shall no longer defile, neither they, nor their kings, by their whoredom, nor by the carcasses of their kings in their altars.*
>
> *In their setting of their threshold by my threshold, and their post by my post, and a wall between me and them, they have even defiled my holy name by their abominations that they have committed; therefore I have consumed them in my anger. Now let them put away their whoredom, and the carcasses of their kings, far from me, and I will dwell in the midst of them forever* (Ezekiel 43:7-9).

*They place their threshold next to my threshold and their posts beside my posts . . .* In other words, where entering over the threshold was supposed to mean a decision to serve God and be surrendered only to Him, they had established their abominations, thus giving the temple a dual purpose. Some went to the temple to worship God, and others went to the same place to worship idols. God gave them many warnings and had patience for hundreds of years, but He finally destroyed Solomon's temple because he could not co-exist with the perversion that was going on.

After the return of a remnant of Jews from Babylon, the temple was rebuilt under Ezra and Nehemiah. Although it appears that this rebuilt temple was never the scene of the same type of idolatry that caused the destruction of Solomon's temple, by the time Christ came, the moneychangers had taken over the temple. They were using God's name and God's house to make money. People came from all over the world to make their offerings, and they had rules and regulations about changing money into the right currency. The moneychangers made commissions on the exchanges and the offerings and sacrifices that had to be bought. There was a lot of money to be made in the temple.

Note: It was immediately after Jesus overthrew the moneychangers in the temple (for the second time in His ministry) that the same people who had welcomed him on Palm Sunday decided to crucify him several days later. When given the opportunity, they chose Barabbas, the robber, instead of Christ, the Messiah. Soon after this, the temple was destroyed for the second and final time.

Before King Josiah made his reforms during what were probably the first seven years of the prophet Jeremiah's ministry, there was not a single copy of the Scriptures (of the Law of the Lord) in the land. Then one day a priest and a scribe were counting the money in the temple, and mixed in with the money, they found the book of the law. One of them took it to the king and said, "We found this book."

King Josiah read the "book," rent his garments and said, *Great is the Lord's anger that is poured out on us because our fathers have not kept the word of the Lord; they have not acted in accordance with all that is written in this book.* (2 Chronicles 34:21). But apparently the scribe and the priest could not have cared less. After decades without God's written Word, they finally found this "book" mixed in with the money. It had somehow become lost in the temple treasury (of all places) (2 Chronicles 34:14).

This is exactly where the Word of the Lord is in many churches and organizations today. It is mixed in with the money. The Word of the Lord is being used to make money. Some men have made lots and lots of money by using God's name. Famous preachers have led many to the Lord, but have mixed money with the things of the Lord. It's not just the television evangelists who can be tempted in this manner. It's not just the big name preachers. It's not just the pastors of huge churches and large congregations. Each and every one of us will be tested and tried. We all have an inherent tendency toward hypocrisy, toward doing one thing in public and another thing in private.

Someone said that the true test of our character is what we do when we think no one is looking (of course, God is looking all the time). If you want to find out how your children really act and where they are in their character, observe them when they don't think you're watching. God is aware of us all the time and can constantly evaluate our character. I think many of us grieve His Holy Spirit continually because of things we do when we think no one is watching.

The Sermon on the Mount then addresses worry (Matthew 6:25-34). I think one of the primary obstacles that stops Christians from doing and being what God wants them to be is worry. This is especially true among the ladies. It seems to be a besetting sin among women to get caught up with worries and anxieties. "What if, and what if such and such were to happen," and all kinds of thoughts like this.

When my parents were making preparations to come to Colombia as Bible translators, my mother was beset with worries all starting with "what if." What if one of the children get sick? What if no one sends us any money? What if I get pregnant down there? She finally saw this as an attack of the enemy.

She envisioned these thoughts as *fiery darts of the wicked one* (Ephesians 6:16), with the "what if" like a little arrowhead at the beginning of each one. Just as she was about to give in to despair and quit trying to follow the Lord to the mission field, she saw that the answer was the *shield of faith*. Every time one of those thoughts came, she would raise the shield of faith, saying, "The Lord will take care of it." The mental attacks soon ended. However, when we actually got to Colombia, most of the things she had worried so much about really did happen to us, and the Lord gloriously took care of us through it all.

Men have strong tendencies to sin in other areas, being more susceptible in the area of sexual fantasies and such. It is not cut and dried however. Men and women both can be tempted in any area. But with worry, fear, impure thoughts, and wrong thinking, we will miss opportunity after opportunity to be effective for God. If our thoughts are not what God wants them to be, we will not be able to speak the right word at the right time when God wants us to be able to minister to someone or deal with a problem. We will not be on the right wave length. By the time we get things figured out and get our act together, it may be too late.

Satan will try to sucker us into his traps with thoughts that may be true, but are the wrong thoughts at the wrong time; thoughts that God does not want to have dominating our minds. The Lord wants us to be thinking about doing His will, right now, today. He wants us to be thinking about what He is thinking about. When our thoughts begin to stray, it becomes a battle for control of our minds. The Lord wants us to submit to His mind and to His thoughts. Harmful, false teaching is abundantly available in the area of meditation and mind control. Most of these programs are expensive and start by encouraging the person to empty their mind and concentrate, which can lead to interaction with and domination by evil spirits. Jesus wants to freely fill our minds with His thoughts and ideas, if we will accept Him.

After He is finished with the subject of worry, Jesus proceeds to judging. The first place we begin to judge others is normally in our thoughts. We see something; we misconstrue the evidence a little bit and begin to make a judgment against someone. This is easy when we do not have all of the facts, and we are not able to look into the other person's heart. We cannot understand the other person's motives. We are called upon by the Lord to give the other person's motives the benefit of the doubt. There are cases where we need to make a judgment based on "rotten fruit" or "wolves in sheep's clothing." But when this person is our brother or sister in Christ and the Lord has placed us into fellowship with that person, we are not to judge their heart or condemn their motives. Any accusation brought against a Christian leader needs to be sustained by two or three witnesses (1 Timothy 5:19).

I found that even with those who had declared themselves to be my enemies, such as the communist guerrillas or people in positions of power who tried to thwart our evangelistic campaigns and ministry, it would still be wrong to judge the motives of their hearts. There is no doubt that they are confused and are producing bitter fruit. In many cases there is no doubt they are our enemies. But the Lord has asked us to love our enemies and be kind to those who persecute us, to pray for them, turn the other cheek and go the extra mile. All of these proven battle tactics are written in the Sermon on the Mount.

As Christians, there is a deception that the enemy would like to place upon us. He would like to trap us into one of two errors. The first is closing off our hearts and rejecting anyone who is wrong, who has hurt us or who is causing us a problem, and leave them no place in our heart. The second is to think that maybe our enemies are really our friends, opening up and intimately trusting people whose hearts are not right with God. Jesus says:

> Give not that which is holy unto the dogs, neither cast ye your pearls before swine, lest they trample them under their feet and turn again and rend you (Matthew 7:6).

This is a severe warning. When the Jews were offering their sacrifices, one of the most sacrilegious things that could happen was for someone to take a sacred piece of the sacrifice and give it to one of the dogs, who would be right there after the meat. Of course, pigs were an unclean animal, and the Jews have always appreciated things of great value, so to give their pearls to swine was the height of squandering resources in their eyes.

Before we share intimate experiences of great value, we need to be sure we are sharing them with the right people. There are intimate things that have happened in our lives and secret things we know of in other people's lives that can be true, but if we share them with the wrong people, we will cause more harm than good. Certain truths need to be kept in reserve, things that we may know that a person of integrity would not betray to someone else. Truth is a two-edged sword that may be used to heal or to destroy. It keeps coming back to integrity. Integrity is the watchword. This is what God wants to develop in each one of us. He wants to form integrity in our character.

After Jesus finishes telling us not to worry about the things of this world, He says, *Take therefore no thought for the morrow, for the morrow shall take thought for the things of itself.* Right before that He said that our heavenly Father knows what we need. Then He says, *Seek ye first the kingdom of God and His righteousness, and all these things shall be added unto you.* Again, it is a question of priorities. It is so easy to get bogged down with the needs and priorities of this world.

One thing greatly complicates matters in our present day

and age which Jesus did not need to point out so strongly at that time (because everyone already understood the clear teaching of the Law in its regard). The Law of the Jews and the writings of the prophets are against usury, the lending of money at high interest rates. It was considered to be quite an abomination. They could lend money at interest to a Gentile, but not among their own people. Their own economic system was not based on interest, banking as we know it today.

One of the principle things that causes a lot of worry about tomorrow is when we are in debt. The more the debt, the greater the worry. I know many people who would like to serve God; they would like to help with God's work, but they cannot spare a cent because their monthly budget is already tied up. They have their house payment, car payment, credit card payments, loan payments and charge accounts at the major department stores. Even gas is bought with a credit card. The interest is incredible. Our entire economic system in America could collapse because it is not based on reality; instead, is leveraged into place by credit. For every dollar bill that is issued by the government in the United States or Canada, the commercial banks can theoretically lend ten or twelve times that much.

What happens if the whole thing starts to cave in and collapse? Where is that going to put the people who have their faith in money, or the stock market, or their savings account? They might wake up some morning, and everything they have placed their trust in could be gone. But if our faith is in the Lord, and we invest our earthly treasures in what He wants, in His kingdom, He will always be here. With Him, you can get a most wonderful return on your investment.

I cannot think of a better place to invest time, resources, or money than in the kingdom of God, seeking after His righteousness. Remember that righteousness also means justice. It means doing and being what God thinks is right. If you spend your time worrying about how to be the kind of person that God wants you to be, and how to do the work that God wants you to do with the gifts and resources He has given you, the Lord will supply your needs. When the world's economic system goes under, you need not go under. There might not be money to throw up on the ceiling, but the Lord will supply and will bring you through. I have had God's providence proven in my life time and time again.

One of the most difficult things for me was to get out of debt and stay out of debt. I had some problems years ago trying to run the ministry on borrowed money. I borrowed more money than I would have borrowed just for myself because it was for the ministry. I was going to do great things for God, and God was going to help me pay it back. Except that God did not feel this way. So when I got into debt, and the Lord did not miraculously help me pay it back, I was really shaken. I had to work to pay it back. It took me years to get out of debt.

After that one major mistake of getting into debt, I decided the Lord did not want me to have credit cards anymore, so I got rid of them and paid them off. But temptations would continue to come along. There would be something wonderful that I could do for the Lord, but I just did not have quite enough money. There would be a way to write a postdated check, or to borrow some money. Every time I have done this, with one or two exceptions where the Lord led me to do it and approved of it, I got myself into sticky and painful messes.

The Lord was trying to teach me about not being in bondage to credit, not selling myself into slavery, not getting myself into a position where I wouldn't be available to Him if He wanted to lead or guide me some other way. He did not want me locked in and unable to move. I have had many people come to me and say, "You know, I would like to serve the Lord full time, but I've got my house payment, this payment or that payment, and I just can't. Who would make all the payments if I were to really go out and serve God?"

I am not saying we have to totally abstain from all credit to have the Lord's blessing, but I believe God wants to be consulted first before those of us who belong to Him get into debt. Each debt is a form of slavery, and Jesus has made it clear that no man can serve two masters. When I promised the Lord, "Lord, I will never borrow another cent unless I ask for and obtain Your approval first," He did not authorize me to borrow another cent for the longest time. I had been addicted to credit. At one point, in order to pay one loan, I had to take out another one. It was like being addicted to drugs. It was terrible. Many Christians are addicted to debt and spend the best part of their lives feeding banks, insurance companies, and finance companies because the interest adds up and up and up. These companies are making a killing off God's people.

The Word of the Lord is very clear. It says that if we follow Him, obey His commands, and do what He tells us to do, then we will not be the ones borrowing money; we will be the ones who are lending money to those who do not know Him. He wants us to be the head and not the tail. God has not declared a law against borrowing and lending He says, *Give to him who asks of you and do not turn away from the one who wants to borrow from you*, but He wants it in the proper order. He wants us to be the ones who have the resources because we have His blessing; we can be the ones who are lending to people who are in need. He wants them to be subservient to us, not us subservient to them.

In the Bible, God makes it clear that the borrower is the servant of the lender; the slave of the lender (Proverbs 22:7). Today we do not believe in slavery, but many people still live in slavery. They have sold themselves into financial slavery, an economic bondage. This is a sad way to live as a Christian. If you are in the position of worrying about your finances not having enough for this or that, or how to make your next credit card payment, I suggest you go over every detail of your finances before the Lord and make a commitment to Him that you are not going to borrow or spend another cent unless He approves. Commit to consult Him prior to each and every financial transaction you make. If there are credit cards or debts bogging you down and holding you back from being free to trust Him, you want to start paying these off and getting rid of them. You want Him to help you get to a position of doing the lending, not the borrowing.

The Lord wants to turn this around. I believe that if we obey God with our finances, when the economic collapse comes, and we are where God wants us to be, we will be the ones who will be reaping the benefits when everyone else is going under. Resources will be falling into our hands instead of us being the ones that are losing everything in the crash.

If you study the great economic crashes of the past, many lost everything, but certain people gained everyone else's wealth because when everything became cheap, the ones who were solvent and had the resources went out and bought it all up. There were tremendous fortunes made at the same time that lots of people lost their shirts. The ones who were heavily leveraged into debt never came out. They were the ones jumping off buildings and committing suicide.

We need to make sure that we are where God wants us to be. I do not think that this is a message that we are to store up goods or horde or anything like that. I am saddened to hear Christian fear mongers say we should bury gold under our refrigerators or hoard up seven years of provisions so we can make it through the tribulation. What God wants is for us to handle our resources and finances according to His will. He wants to be in charge. He wants to use us to help meet the needs of others around us. If we start hanging on to things, it bottlenecks God's economy.

When we are free with our resources (not to the point of getting into debt), we can say, "Here I am, Lord, and what I have is Yours. How do You want it used?" We can live without fear of tomorrow, and the Lord can begin to bless. He can bless others through us, and others can see God in us. They can feel His hand. Then He can prosper and protect us. How are we to overcome evil with good, if we selfishly hoard our resources? God doesn't want His people to retreat, or even to circle their wagons. He wants to lead them to battle and win the victory.

So what are we to pray for when we pray? One of the things we are supposed to do when we pray is listen to the Lord. This is something many Christians do not do. We are told not to pray like the pagans who think that they will be heard because of their many words. When we pray, God wants to talk to us. We can express ourselves to Him and share what is on our hearts and minds, but we need to listen to the Lord. We need to begin our prayer with *Our Father, Who art in heaven.* Not a singular personal pronoun, but a collective pronoun. Our Father. We should be as concerned about the needs of those around us as we are about our own needs. God is not pleased with the selfish prayers that many of us pray.

If your children come to you continually to ask for things for themselves, always for something more, you get a bit tired of it. But what if your child was concerned about those around him (or her), and every time he came with a petition, it was for some other needy child? What would your concept be of your child? Would it touch your heart as well, and would you be interested in helping your child help those around him? This should be something you want to implement in your child's life. This is the way I think God feels when we come to Him with the needs of those around us, putting the needs of others first.

*Ask, and it shall be given you; seek, and ye shall find; knock, and it shall be opened unto you; for every one that asks receives, and he that seeks finds, and to him that knocks it shall be opened* (Matthew 7:7-8).

The Greek verb in the original language denotes continuous action that is an attribute of the person. We do not have that tense in English, but it would be like saying *For everyone who is an asker, receives; everyone who is a seeker, finds; to everyone who is a knocker, the door will be opened.* There is a quality of perseverance, but not perseverance after the things of the world. Jesus is talking about asking, seeking and knocking for (setting our sights on) the real wealth and riches that God has to offer: wisdom, understanding, discernment, the fruit of the Holy Spirit, and His gifts. All the valuable things that He wants to endow us with are available to those who persistently set their hearts to follow Him and go after His best.

God will not cast His pearls before swine. He will not throw what is sacred to the dogs. He will not share His wisdom, understanding and intimate secrets of the kingdom with those who are unworthy. He will not throw precious pearls of truth out for anyone who superficially wants to know about them. If you really want to be used of God, it will take persistence on your part: asking, seeking, and knocking.

*Or what man is there of you, whom, if his son asks for bread, will he give him a stone? Or if he asks for fish, will he give him a serpent? If ye then, being evil, know how to give good gifts unto your children, how much more shall your Father who is in the heavens give good things to those that ask him?*

*Therefore, all things whatsoever ye desire that men should do unto you, so also shall ye do unto them, for this is the law and the prophets* (Matthew 7:9-12).

Again, it comes back to righteousness (being and doing what God wants) in our relationship with those around us, in the same manner that we would want others to do unto us. We can always know how God would want us to treat someone else because we can put ourselves in that person's position and know how we would want to be treated under the same circumstances.

Many of those calling themselves Christians do not seek what is righteous. They make a case for going their own way, but they feel a little guilt in their conscience. Then to get another stamp of approval or get out from under responsibility, they come in for counseling. They will seek the pastor or counselor to reinforce the humanistic rationale that they have made up for themselves.

It is amazing to see the number of men who come in for family counseling because their wife needs to be straightened out. Or if it's the wife, then the husband needs to be straightened out. If it's the parents, then the children need straightening out. They are always looking for someone else to straighten out their loved one. The meetings we had in Colombia focused on the area of family reconciliation. Everyone has family problems. Everyone has someone in their family they feel needs to be straightened out. So if we advertised in our meetings there would be lots of good advice on the family, people would come in, not so much because they thought they personally needed anything, but because they had this poor soul in their family they had to get straightened out.

God looks at things from a different perspective. He says in verse 13,

*Enter ye in at the narrow gate, for the way that leads to destruction is wide and spacious, and those who follow it are many; because narrow is the gate, and confined*

B lessed are the peacemakers, for they shall be called the sons of God. This is the focal point of the Beatitudes. It represents the purpose of Jesus' ministry here on this earth. One of His main objectives in coming here is that we might be called the sons of God. Notice it does not say Blessed are the peacemakers, for they shall call themselves the sons of God. It says Blessed are the peacemakers, for they shall be called the sons of God. This is similar to when the word "Christian" was first used to describe the followers of Christ in Antioch, because they were like Him.

If the Beatitudes have been planted in our hearts, and we have honestly set our will to follow God, He can begin to work in and through us. It will become apparent to those around us that we are indeed the sons of God. "Sons," in this usage, in the original language, has no gender. This beatitude also implies that God will call us His sons.

In the Christian world that we live in today (even in the non-Christian world of other religions), many people call themselves sons of God. In a certain context in the past even Satan was included in this. In the book of Job it says that the sons of God were gathered, and Satan was among them (Job 1:6). In other words, there have been times when it has been convenient for Satan to identify himself as a son of God. The fact that someone identifies himself as a son of God is not the important thing. The important thing is what we are in God's eyes. Who are the ones that He identifies as His sons?

*Keep yourselves also from the false prophets, who come to you in sheep's clothing, but inwardly they are ravening wolves. Ye shall know them by their fruits. Do men gather grapes of thorns, or figs of thistles? Even so every good tree brings forth good fruit, but a corrupt tree brings forth evil fruit. A good tree cannot bring forth evil fruit, neither can a corrupt tree bring forth good fruit* (Matthew 7:15-18).

There is a bit of confusion on the last phrase of this Scripture due to difficulties involved in translating it into the English language. I have studied this passage word by word and phrase by phrase. What this Scripture means to me is that a good tree is a healthy tree. A corrupt tree is a rotten tree. You can have two trees of the same species, two apple trees for instance, and one of them is rotten to the core and the other is sound and healthy. The Lord is saying that just as you cannot get grapes from thorn bushes or figs from thistles, you cannot get good healthy fruit from a rotten fruit tree. A rotten apple tree will produce scraggly, rotten, little apples. A good or healthy tree will produce wholesome, delicious fruit. The old man has his roots (nature) in Adam. The new man is firmly rooted in Christ.

I have a friend in Canada who races sled dogs. I commented on how friendly his dogs were in comparison to some other people's sled dogs. Then he told me his secret. At an early age (around 28 days I believe), the dogs imprint psychologically. If the puppies are around friendly people at that time, they will be imprinted by them and be friendly for the rest of their lives towards humans. If they are around a mother dog that is aloof, withdrawn, and distrustful, then that is what they become. So, at the critical time, my friend takes all the pups into his cabin and has his kids play with them. To my knowledge, he has never had a mean dog. This principle is very important in Christian-home run or when something spectacular happens. Do they remember every throw to the first baseman? No, but if he drops the ball they remember it.

If our hearts are pure before God, if His presence and peace are there in our lives, no matter what kind of wild pitch we are served, we will respond in a godly manner. Our natural reaction will be godly because our innermost being is filled with God and with His power. I used to wish when ugly things happened or when difficult problems occurred, if only I could have a few minutes to get away by myself to kneel down, pray, seek the Lord, and find out how to respond. It is when I am in an emergency, and I have to make a snap decision that what I really am inside is exposed for all to see. Do I fly off the handle and shoot from the hip, or is the peace of God still in control?

This life is a training ground. This life is an opportunity to practice for the reality that is to come. At the end of the Sermon on the Mount, it says *whosoever hears these words of mine and does them...* The word "hears" implies the connotation of someone who is in direct contact with the Lord and thus receives the grace to comply with what God says.

*Whosoever commits sin transgresses also the law: for sin is the transgression of the law. And ye know that he appeared to take away our sins, and there is no sin in him. Whosoever abides in him does not sin: whosoever sins has not seen him or known him.*

*Little children, let no one deceive you; he that does righteousness is righteous, even as he also is righteous. He that commits sin is of the devil; for the devil sins from the beginning. For this purpose the Son of God appeared, that he might undo the works of the devil.*

*Whosoever is born of God does not commit sin; for his seed remains in him; and he cannot sin, because he is born of God. In this the sons of God are manifest, and the sons of the devil: whosoever does not righteousness and that loves not his brother is not of God* (1 John 3:4-10).

This is a very intriguing passage that used to bother me a lot. Here the apostle John is using the word for sin, *hamartia*, and is saying that if we belong to God, we cannot sin. Have you wondered about that one? How in the world can we not sin, yet none of us is perfect, and all of us are doing things from time to time that need to be repented of and set right. Some people have taken these verses and built a doctrine of sinless perfection: that once we have this encounter with the Lord, no matter what we do, it is not sin. This is a terrible heresy.

Again we need to examine the terms. Language is not constant; it can shift with time. The way that I have come to understand this passage is by looking at the term translated sin. There are several. This term comes from a Greek word that has to do with consistently shooting at the wrong target or goal. It does not just mean "to miss the mark." The person could score a perfect bull's-eye, and it would still be sin (*hamartia*) if the archer was aiming at the wrong target.

The way I have understood this is that if we belong to the Lord, if we have Him inside of us, and He is in control of our innermost being, we will no longer be shooting at the wrong target. We will no longer have the wrong goals. We will no longer fill our lives with the love of money, greed, selfishness or feeding of our pride. We will not be aiming at fulfilling our own desires. We will be aiming for the righteousness of God. We will be aiming for the perfection of God. We are talking about training and target practice in this life. We may not be hitting the target perfectly or even consistently. Every time we shoot, it may not be a perfect bull's-eye, but at least we will be aiming at the right target instead of the wrong target. I believe that this is the sense in which John says that when we are in Christ, we cannot sin. He is talking about our goals and ambitions, not absolute sinless perfection overriding our humanity.

There is a certain sense in which we will never get 100 percent on every math test. We will never be able to perfectly remember everything we said or did. I can tell someone to meet me at 5:00 a.m., forget, and not get there because I am human. Or, I can deliberately try to mislead someone and tell them I will be there when I am not even intending to go. Here are two situations that are as different as apples and oranges. The one is due to my humanity; the other is a deliberate transgression that will interrupt my intimate fellowship with God and needs to be repented of before God and the person that I mislead.

When I make a human mistake or failing, it is still necessary to make rectification with the person that I have offended. If I say to someone, "I will meet you here at 5:00 a.m.," and my alarm clock does not go off, or I forget, or oversleep or am delayed, it is not a deliberate transgression that will separate me from fellowship with God.

The situation, however, between me and the individual I have inconvenienced needs to be cleared up. I need to say, "I'm sorry I didn't make it. This and that happened, and I'll try and do better next time." There is a difference between a willful transgression which will cloud our hearts and interrupt our intimate communion with the Lord, and a mistake that comes from our human limitations.

*Blessed are the peacemakers, for they shall be called the sons of God.* They are the ones who radiate peace because the Prince of Peace is on the throne of their lives. This is the goal. This is what God is after. We are to be His ambassadors. We are to represent Him, and He is the Prince of Peace. When He is in control of our lives, we can face the most difficult circumstance or go through the worst conflict, and His peace will never leave us because He says *I will never leave you, nor forsake you.*

One of the ways God has led and guided me is precisely through that peace. Whenever His peace is interrupted in my heart, when something has affected the presence of God inside of me, I know it is time to get off by myself on my knees before the Lord and not leave until the Lord has put His finger on whatever is not right. It could have been something I said, did, failed to do, thought, or was planning to do. God wants to head us off at the pass and stop us before we can implement wrong elements into our lives. He wants to stop us before those ugly words can even come out of our mouths, before we have to go and straighten out what we said or did. He would like us to be so sensitive to His presence that we can detect it when we are just at the beginning stage of wrong thoughts, feelings, or motivation and allow Him to stop and correct us before we miss His perfect will and end up hurting ourselves or someone else.

If we have already messed things up, our error can be rectified because those around us, especially our families, all need examples. My dad used to tell me that a human life can never be totally wasted. If for nothing else, it can always serve as a bad example for everyone else. So even when we are a bad example, our lives can be used to the glory of God if we are willing to submit to Him and do what He wants us to do, which is to ask for forgiveness and allow Him to deal with our pride as we go to whomever we have wronged to set it straight. Many times we can gain more ground for the kingdom of God by setting an example of repentance and true submission to God than by anything else we could do or say. Our mistakes and failures are golden opportunities to demonstrate to those around us what real repentance and submission to Jesus Christ is.

A significant number of people have a problem truly repenting and submitting to God without seeing an example in actual practice. I found that the guerrillas who captured me had no concept of repentance. But when I started admitting when I was wrong, some of them came down from their high horses and started admitting when they were wrong. Before I left, one of them, with tears in his eyes, asked me to forgive him. These were the same guys who at the beginning stood there and belligerently said, "We don't make mistakes. Everybody else makes mistakes, but we don't make mistakes."

Have you ever been around someone who does not make mistakes? I have had parents bring their children in for counseling and say, "This kid will never admit when he makes a mistake." When I started asking them questions, it became evident that the father never made mistakes either. Our attitude will be imprinted on those who are around us. One bad apple can spoil the whole barrel. One conflictive person loose in a church or work place can sour the atmosphere for everyone else. The conflictive spirit they have wreaks havoc all over the place. The reverse is also true. One person generating God's peace can have a profound impact on those all around. A little salt can preserve and flavor a whole container of food.

God's peace is contagious. We can go around infecting people with it just as if we had a transmittable disease. When our attitude is right, it speaks much louder than what we say. If we want to be effective for the Lord, we need to have two things right. We need to have our attitude (our heart) right, while at the same time our doctrine (our mental knowledge) also needs to be correct. But it is definitely better to have someone whose heart is right before God, even if their doctrine is not completely straight, than someone whose mental knowledge of doctrine is perfect when their heart is rotten.

To compare this with aviation, most techniques of good pilotage have to do with obtaining and maintaining the proper flight attitude of the aircraft. You cannot do precision maneuvers or fly a precise instrument approach unless you can control the attitude of the airplane through all three axes. This is especially true in short-field flying. Someone who cannot control the attitude of the airplane will overshoot or undershoot and could have a serious accident. Fledgling pilots should not go anywhere near a short field until they can dominate the attitude of the aircraft.

On the other hand, it is also necessary to know all about the mechanical systems and about navigation. A good pilot needs to know many things, and he needs to know them so well that in an emergency he will act upon the proper information. Tragic accidents have occurred because something failed on the airplane, and the pilot could not remember if it had to do with the electrical system or with the hydraulic system, and he disabled the wrong system causing more problems. Pilots with lightning reflexes have had an engine failure and shut down their good engine thinking they were shutting down the one that had failed. It is not necessarily the gifted person with the lightning reflexes who makes the best pilot in a crisis; rather it is the one who calmly, instinctively, does the right thing while under pressure.

This holds true in Christianity as well. When we do not know what to do and are under pressure to make a snap judgment or decision, and we do not have the peace of the Lord, the best thing we can do is stop, seek the Lord and find out what He wants rather than go off and make a quick decision we may live to regret later on.

I would like to suggest that you use the Beatitudes like a checklist. In every aircraft there are always checklists. There are pilots who think they do not need the checklist; they think they can do it on their own. Everything goes fine until they forget some important item, like coming in for a landing without putting the landing gear (wheels) down first. Many beautiful (and expensive) airplanes have been crunched into the asphalt, destroying the propeller, damaging the engine, sometimes even generating an explosion or fire, because the pilots forgot this simple procedure.

God wants us to check some important things. The Scriptures are clear on this. When someone speaks on behalf of the Lord, whether in teaching, preaching, or music ministry, there should be the opportunity for those with spiritual discernment to evaluate what has happened and compare anything questionable with the written, revealed Word of God. It is not just some hotshot saying, "Thus saith the Lord," and nobody can question him. There are people in every part of the body of Christ who have gifts of discernment and wisdom from the Lord. They will normally not be your outgoing, charismatic type of personalities. These are people who would rather be in the background, people with true servant's hearts who are not self-assertive. They need to be drawn out, and their gifts need to be cultivated. Their gifts are important, and they balance the others who are gung-ho.

If you are a gifted individual, go over the Beatitudes and make sure that what you are doing is in line with Jesus' teaching. Go over the first one. When I use my gift, am I feeding my pride? Is it an ego trip for me to be able to stand up and minister to (or entertain) others? If it is, you are headed for trouble. Sooner or later, Satan will trip you up, and you will fall flat on your face. Is your gift in submission to the Lord, to do His will and only His will? Do you use your gift with fear and trembling? You do not want to hold back anything that God wants to express through you, but at the same time, you do not want to say anything more than what He wants. Or are you using your gift to play games and impose your will on others?

There are people who use their God-given gifts to play spiritual parlor games. This is not what they are for. I have been to prayer meetings where there was a "Can you top this?" spirit, and many were on an ego trip. Even leadership can fall into the trap of using a "Thus saith the Lord," approach when they really want to impose their own will on somebody. Guess what happens when this kind of thing develops? The glory, power and blessing of the Lord starts leaving. What begins in the spirit should not end in the flesh. Worse yet, Satan can come in with a spirit of deception and substitute the true spirit with a false spirit, and those that are promoting their own glory will not even know when the Spirit of the Lord left them. This happened to King Saul. He ended up consulting the witch of Endor.

In Jeremiah's day, numerous false prophets prophesied whatever the people wanted to hear. Nobody wanted to listen to the true prophet because it was uncomfortable. I have a friend who says that although one of the main goals of the church is to comfort the afflicted, if the ministry of the church does not afflict the comfortable, it will ultimately lose the blessing of God.

*Blessed are those that mourn, for they shall be comforted.* Are you using your gift out of a soft, contrite, humble heart before the Lord, sensitive to the concerns and needs of those around you, sensitive to your own need to be led by God's Spirit? Or do you feel self-sufficient because you are so educated, qualified, or talented?

*Blessed are those who hunger and thirst for righteousness, for they shall be satisfied.* Do you hunger and thirst for being and doing what God wants, for treating people right. Or do you just want to be treated right yourself? Do you get your feathers ruffled when somebody doesn't treat you right? Or are you filled with a hunger and thirst for treating other people justly? When Jesus is in control, "how am I being treated..." is no longer important, but rather "how am I treating others?"

When you think, "I didn't treat that person right. I didn't do right by them," does it bother you? If it does, you cannot what our gifts are for; they are to edify the collective body of Christ (His church) (Ephesians 4:11-13).

It is tragic that powerful gifts of evangelism have been given to individuals with power from God to persuade men to turn to God, but if the evangelist uses his gift to persuade people to give money to himself and to his ministry, the next thing you know, the salt has lost its savor, and it is being trampled underfoot by men.

Satan can quote from the Bible too. He took Jesus to the top of the temple and said *If thou art the Son of God, cast thyself down, for it is written, He shall give his angels charge concerning thee, and in their hands they shall bear thee up lest at any time thou dash thy foot against a stone.* Satan will quote Scripture. He will try anything to appeal to our pride. When he quotes Scripture to us, we need to identify the source of the message. Just the fact that it is a Bible reference that can be pulled out of context and applied does not mean that God is speaking to us. It must be God. Jesus answered Satan with another Scripture. *It is written again, Thou shalt not tempt the Lord thy God.*

Satan wanted Him to say, "Ok, I'm Superman. Here I go off the pinnacle of the temple." God is not looking for superstars. He is looking for the humble and contrite in spirit who tremble at His word (Isaiah 66:2).

Jesus did not use His gifts to build His own pride. When He did something miraculous like healing somebody or raising a little girl from the dead, He would say, "Don't tell anybody. Give the glory to God but don't say it was Me." This contrasts sharply with some of our modern day ministries that deal in signs and wonders.

The last temptation was "I'll show you all the kingdoms of the world. Just bow down and acknowledge me, and they're Yours. You don't have to die on the cross. You don't have to give Your life. You can have it all without any sacrifice, pain, or suffering." Satan still offers us that temptation. You can have everything. You're a son of the King. Nothing is too good for you. You don't have to deny yourself. You don't have to pay a price or suffer. You can have everything. Just name it and claim it because you are a King's kid. Jesus rejected that offer and continued His walk in humility. He said *Foxes have holes, and the birds of the heaven have nests, but the Son of Man has not where to lay his head.* He also said *And whosoever does not bear his stake (cross) and come after me cannot be my disciple.*

There are many people calling themselves disciples of Christ, claiming to be sons of God, but the ones who are truly the sons of God are those who take up their cross and follow the Lord wherever He goes. But He says *My yoke is easy and my burden is light.* His cross is a joy because nothing can compare with the peace only He can give.

God's peace is a direct result of the projection of His power. Think of the tremendous power that holds the universe together, yet this is just a tiny fraction of His might. His power is available to the sons of God, power that can enable them to project and radiate His peace. The day is coming when Jesus Christ will be revealed in all His glory. The Bible says that all creatures groan and strain waiting for the manifestation (unveiling) of the sons of God (Romans 8:19-23). When that great day comes, God's sons won't just radiate peace; they will enforce peace. All creation will be brought back into harmony with God, and we (His sons) will be joint-heirs with Jesus Christ (Romans 8:17).

*Blessed are the peacemakers, for they shall be called the sons of God.* What do people call you? What does God call you?

> *For if ye live according to the flesh ye shall die, but if through the Spirit ye mortify the deeds of the body ye shall live. For all that are led by the Spirit of God, the same are sons of God. For ye have not received*

*the spirit of bondage to be in fear again, but ye have received the Spirit of adoption of sons, whereby we cry, Abba, Father. For the same Spirit bears witness unto our spirit that we are sons of God, and if sons, also heirs certainly of God and joint-heirs with Christ, if so be that we suffer with him that we may be also glorified together with him.*

*For I know with certainty that the sufferings of this present time are not worthy to be compared with the coming glory which shall be manifested in us. For the earnest hope of the creatures waits for the manifestation of the sons of God. For the creatures were subjected to vanity, not willingly, but by reason of him who has subjected them, with the hope that the same creatures shall be delivered from the bondage of corruption into the glorious liberty of the sons of God* (Romans 8:13-21).

LET US PRAY:

*Heavenly Father, we want You to call us Your sons. Lord, clear away all our own ideas that we have about ourselves. We want to know what You think about us. We want to know who we are in Your eyes. Can those who are around us see You in us? Is Your character imprinted on us? Are we each and every day becoming more and more like you? Or are we like a fruit tree that is rotten at the core, producing scraggly little fruit that gets worse each year? What kind of fruit are we producing?*

*Lord, help us to produce healthy, wholesome fruit. Help us to lead others to You and see them go on to a healthy, wholesome walk with You. May they in turn produce good fruit so the world can look at us and see Your image in us, which will inspire them with hope and plant a desire for You in their hearts. May we be tantalizing to the world like a beautiful, delicious apple on a fruit tree that anyone would be delighted in eating, rather than being so rotten and full of worms that no one can stand to partake of what we are offering in Your name, and they spit out the bite they have taken.*

*Lord, help us. We repent of all the things we have done our own way, trying to do Your work our way and all the mistakes we have made, errors we have perpetrated, and wrong attitudes we have expressed. We repent of all the things we have done in Your name that were not really in Your name but in our own name.*

*Lord, we want to get back to the cross, back to letting You pick the good ideas, back to using our gifts for others to bring them into a proper relationship with Yourself, to edify Your body.*

*Lord, please deliver us from using the gifts and abilities that you have given us to build our pride, our ego, our name, or even the name of our collective group. Please deliver us from using the gifts you have given us to line our own pockets or to raise up our own little kingdoms in your name. We want to use our gifts to exalt Your Name; we want to lift You up so that You might draw all men to Yourself. To reach others and rescue them from the kingdom of darkness, sacrifices are involved; but You tell us that to obey is better than sacrifice. Please deliver Your people from sacrificing things You never told them to sacrifice. Let our sacrifices be pleasant in Your sight that we may sacrifice only that which is pleasing and agreeable to You.*

*Lord, we wish that those who are in the world around us could look at us and say, "They surely must be the people of God, because look at the blessing. Everything they put their hand to prospers. I wish I could have that blessing. I wish I could be like them." We ask that they will be drawn to us and to You. Lord, please give us Your grace, which is Your power to win the battle in Your Name. We are tired of trying to function in this world without Your power or Your peace. We want to follow behind You, Lord, and witness the power of Your presence in us, your people, overcoming the enemy. We want to go in and possess the land in Your name. We want to see the restoration, the purification of Your people, Your church. We want to win those in darkness away from the tentacles of the enemy. We want to see this nation return to You. Use us, Lord. We want to be a small part of Your great Master Plan.*
*Amen.*

*Blessed are those who suffer persecution for righteousness' sake, for theirs is the kingdom of the heavens.*

The promise on the end of the eighth beatitude is exactly the same as that on the end of the first one. It is as if God designed this whole series of attitudes, promises and blessings to be a loop, and for us to go around and around within the Beatitudes, like going around and around up a spiral staircase.

I have found that the Beatitudes are an excellent check list: When something is wrong in my life, or I need to evaluate my performance in a given area or search for discernment, a good place to look to make sure my life is on a solid footing is the Beatitudes. I need to periodically check to see whether what I am doing is motivated out of pride or out of a humble heart; to see whether I really want my own way by taking the law into my own hands, or if I am truly submitted to the Lordship and will of Jesus Christ. Is the Holy Spirit shining God's truth into my heart and softening it? Or is my heart hardening? Do I hunger and thirst for righteousness, for doing and being what God wants, or is there some other motivation in my heart? Am I truly interested in treating other people the way I want God to treat me, with a merciful attitude? Or is there a root of bitterness beginning to develop in a given relationship or area? Above all, is the peace of God in my heart? Because if it isn't, and I sense that the peace of God has left my heart, the best thing I know to do when this happens is to get down on my knees until the

Lord shows me what is needed to regain His peace. I need to be willing to take whatever steps He would outline to me.

Doing and being what God wants will bring persecution. It will bring opposition from the enemy. Listen to the ninth beatitude:

> *Blessed are ye when men shall revile you and persecute you and shall say all manner of evil against you falsely for my sake. Rejoice and be exceeding glad, for great is your reward in the heavens; for so they persecuted the prophets who were before you.*

Evidence that you are where God wants you to be is if you are receiving persecution. One of Satan's key tactics is to foment lies and rumors. Satan is an expert at starting lies and rumors. If he gets us suckered into defending ourselves against these lies and rumors, defending our reputation, then he can get the upper hand because he gets us to quit hurting him and start defending ourselves, something that we should have placed on the altar before the Lord. If we have entered the spirit of the Beatitudes and the kingdom of God through the narrow gate, our pride and our desire for reputation should have been left far behind.

It is easy to listen to the Beatitudes. They are lovely; they sound wonderful. There is something inside of us that says, "Yes, that is the way it is. This is the way my personal relationships should be." But when we put it into practice, it is like the scroll that the prophet Ezekiel was asked to eat: sweet in his mouth, and bitter in his stomach. Again, the apostle John in Revelation Chapter 10 was asked to eat the same type of scroll, or message. The Sermon on the Mount is like that; it is sweet in our mouth, but it can be bitter in our stomach as we digest it and put it into practice.

Hearing Jesus' teaching starts us on the path to the blessing.

*Therefore, whosoever hears these words of mine and does them,*
*I will liken him unto a prudent man, who built his house upon*
*the rock...* Remember that word for house has a double meaning. It can mean household and family as well as the physical
four walls and a roof. So, the Lord is giving an example of a
house (or of a family) that was built on the rock. The rain came
down, and the streams rose; the winds blew and beat against
that house, yet it did not fall because it had its foundation on
the rock. It is only by putting on Jesus' attitudes, His life, and
His heart through the power and presence of His Holy Spirit
within us and becoming a living example of Jesus and His
message that we build our house on the rock.

I was taught by a well-meaning Sunday School teacher that
just to believe in Jesus was to have my house on the rock. That
is a good start, but the Bible says even the demons believe, and
they tremble with fear (James 2:19). But they do not live according to the Beatitudes, and they do not have the blessing. They
are under a curse. It is not enough to just believe facts about
God in our heads to have our house founded on the rock; we
must hear Jesus' words in order to put his message into practice.
We will make mistakes along the way, and when this happens,
we have to go back to the first beatitude admit our mistakes,
forsake our sin, and leave our pride behind. We must resubmit
the problem areas of our life to the Lord and ask Him to do
a cleansing work within us, starting from the depths of our
heart, to purge us of everything which is not right and to give
us a hunger and thirst to be what He wants us to be and to do
what He wants us to do.

Being is more important than doing. We are in a world that
likes to <u>do</u> things, but God's message to us is that He wants us
to <u>be</u> a certain kind of people. All of the things that we can do
for God will come to an end. Paul says that all these things will
come to an end, but there are three things that will remain:

faith, hope and charity, which is the love of God (1 Corinthians Chapter 13). All three incorporate the Lord Jesus Christ because He is the source of all three. It is our faith in Him, our hope in Him, and the kind of love that only He can plant in us that will endure forever.

Living the ninth beatitude where friends slander us, and the enemy wages a full-blown attack on us, and still be able to continue on the course that God has led us without wavering, but genuinely rejoicing, is difficult. This is not always the case in my life. Many times, when the enemy attacks, and I know the Lord wants me to rejoice, I try to put a smile on my face, but I do not feel like rejoicing inside. You want to know what I have found? When I do not feel like rejoicing because Satan is attacking and slandering me, it is because there is something that is still mine that I am subconsciously clung to that I am afraid I am about to lose. It's MY reputation that is on the line, it's MY ministry, it's MY family; anything that is still mine and has not been placed on the altar of total commitment to Christ will take away my capacity to rejoice in the Lord when I am under attack. Jesus said *For whosoever desires to save his life shall lose it, and whosoever will lose his life for my sake shall find it.*

Defending what is mine has often caused me to stop pressing the enemy the way God wants me to press him and to start defending myself instead. Then Satan is able to obtain enough time to marshal his defenses back up and regroup. Then does he ever counter-attack! It is very subtle. He will try to get us to react by provoking us. He will try to get a reaction out of us by testing, probing and attacking any area that is not totally submitted to God.

Let's turn to the book of James. One of the most misinterpreted Bible verses that I know of is in this book. Have you heard someone (or maybe you've done it yourself) quote this verse to the devil when they are in trouble, and he is attacking: *Resist* must be honest before God and willing to admit our faults and failures, rather than cover them up when God's truth exposes things that are out of place in our lives. When our brother has something against us, we must be willing to go with a humble attitude and do what is necessary to set it right.

It is important that we stick together with those God has placed alongside of us. If Satan can divide us, he can conquer us. He likes to divide and conquer. He likes to attack our character, our integrity, and then question all the virtues that God is building in our lives. If we have not died to the old man, we will react and start defending ourselves. When we put energy into defending ourselves, Satan will get a second wind and be able to regroup. We may not be able to win the battle or obtain the victory that we were trying for. I have seen this happen many times. As we have been going through with our meetings in Colombia, each one has been a battle with demonic forces before we could enter a high school and present the gospel to thousands of young people or before we could go into a city and preach in the churches, or before we could get permission from the civil authorities.

Satan does not give up ground without a fight. He does not want to lose territory. He does not want to lose those whom he has in bondage. He wants to try to take as many people with him as he can and frustrate God's purposes. Maybe he thinks that if he does that, God will let him off the hook. I don't know. But he is not only continuing his full-fledged rebellion against God, he is also trying to get as many people with him as possible. He plays for keeps. When he manages to delude people and sell them a bill of goods, it is a very serious situation when they die. We are all responsible for the truth that we have.

Listen to what James says next:

*Draw near to God, and he will draw near to you.*

*Cleanse your hands, ye sinners; and purify your hearts, ye double minded. Be afflicted and mourn and weep; let your laughter be turned to mourning and your joy to heaviness. Humble yourselves in the sight of the Lord, and he shall lift you up* (James 4:8-10).

This *humble yourselves in the sight of the Lord, and He shall lift you up* comes in the context of spiritual warfare. This is another verse that is quoted out of context all the time as if it should stand alone. But it comes sandwiched right in the middle of how to stand, resist the devil, and put him to flight.

Verse 17 says:

*Therefore sin is still in the one that knows to do good and does not do it.*

Friends, it is possible for us to do battle in the name of the Lord, to win victories and be able to push back the powers of darkness. It is also possible to take things away from the enemy, to bind the strongman and take what is in his house (starting with the people he holds hostage). If the Lord is giving us orders to go into battle, and we do not fight, it is really sin.

A couple of the encounters that we have had on different occasions in Colombia exemplify this. Satan is very subtle. He will try to get our attention diverted. He will try to make you think you do not have time to go after the demon that possesses some person because it will take too long. Maybe you would have to spend weeks praying and fasting in order for that particular demon to come out. You better leave it alone and go on to something easier. But the Lord can give us wisdom and victory in each and every circumstance.

One time we were leaving for a large meeting and were almost out the door. We had tickets for an airplane, and thousands of miners were waiting for us at an emerald mining district. Along came a Catholic priest with a man who was the accuser of the brethren, and that is what he started doing to me in that meeting.

He said, "You thought you were going to do a good job here, didn't you? But you're not. You thought some of these kids were going to come to the Lord, but they're not. You're out of line. What did you just say to that Episcopalian priest at noon?"

I thought, "Yeah, he's a scuba diver, and I have a scuba diving license, and I told him a story about scuba diving." And then I thought, "Oh no. I haven't talked to anyone about scuba diving in a long time, and the story I told him about scuba diving was about 50 percent fact and 50 percent fiction." I didn't do it knowingly. I just told it the last way I had told it years before. The last time I told it was before the Lord had dealt with me about exaggeration. Even then it was a subtle thing. I would not exaggerate 50 percent the first time, just 4 or 5 percent each time I told it, and then the next time I told it, I would make it a bit better, and then a little more. After telling something about ten times, there were whopping lies in it, but I had talked myself into believing my own lies because I had been bringing them up gradually.

So, Satan is telling me, "You deviated from the truth. You exaggerated. God won't bless someone who is lying. You can't possibly expect to stand up there and preach to these kids and have any of them repent. I got you. I got you now, and you're not going to come out of here with anything useful to the Lord."

I felt about an inch tall. I did not want to get up in front of those kids. I just wanted to dig a hole or go out and find some place to have a long time alone between myself and the Lord. Then it occurred to me that I could find the priest, apologize and get it straightened out. But they announced me at that moment. The room was so packed with kids, and he was in the back row while I was in the front. There was no way I could get back there so I had to go up and start speaking. My heart felt like it was as heavy as lead, sitting down at the bottom of my feet some place. I went up there feeling in my heart that I did not have the blessing or the anointing of the Lord.

When I got to the podium, I started out in prayer, and the Lord gave me wisdom as to what to do. I spoke precisely on the importance of the truth and used what had just happened to me as an example. I apologized to the fellow that I had told the exaggeration to right in front of everybody. I faced Satan head on and called his bluff. The Holy Spirit took the consciences of those kids and started to squeeze, and many of them came to a deeper knowledge of the Lord during that time at camp. The Lord broke them wide open. They had a perfect example right in front of them of what they needed to do and how they needed to be honest and sincere and allow the Lord to deal with anything that was not right in their lives.

What Satan meant for a route to win a battle caused him, in fact, to lose the battle. It turned around in a split second, right when I thought it was all lost and was ready to throw in the towel, convinced that nothing could be done. The only thing I could think of was to pray and say, "Lord, I don't know what to do, and if You don't help, we're lost."

This has stuck with me. Many times when I do not know what to preach, and I do not know what to do (just about every meeting and every time I preach), I like to have a little talk with the Lord and say, "Lord, I don't know what to do. If You do not give me a message and direct me precisely as to what You want said and done, it's useless for me to simply get up and tell a bunch of stories that are going to entertain people, so they can say what a wonderful speaker they had, but nobody will come under conviction of sin or be touched by Your Spirit. Nothing of real eternal value will be accomplished unless You lead the way."

To live the Sermon on the Mount means hand to hand

Chapter Seven

In addition to setting a standard for our behavior, each beatitude has a promise at the end. Those who live the Beatitudes are promised all these things: The kingdom of heaven will be theirs, they will be comforted (receive the Comforter, who is the Holy Spirit), they will inherit the earth, they will be filled with righteousness, they will obtain mercy, they will see God, they will be called the sons of God, and they will receive a great reward in heaven.

These marvelous promises are all conditional. We must comply with God's requirements if we expect to attain His blessing. The themes that are central to the Sermon on the Mount are woven throughout virtually every book in the Bible. The prophet Micah said:

> *He has declared unto thee, O man, what is good and what the Lord requires of thee: only to do right judgment, and to love mercy, and to humble thyself to walk with thy God* (Micah 6:8).

These are the same three central requirements of the Beatitudes. 2 Peter Chapter 1 helps to put this in perspective:

> *...as all things that pertain to life and to godliness are given us of his divine power, through the knowledge of him that has called us by his glory and virtue, whereby are given unto us exceeding great and precious promises, that by these ye might be made participants of the divine nature, having fled the corruption that is in the world through lust* (2 Peter 1:3-4).

As you study the Scriptures, note that most of God's promises are conditional. These conditions need to be met in order for us to be able to claim His *exceeding great and precious promises.* Thinking about these conditions, Peter goes on to say:

> *Ye also, giving all diligence to the same, show forth virtue in your faith; and in virtue, knowledge; and in knowledge, temperance; and in temperance, patience; and in patience, fear of God; and in fear of God, brotherly love; and in brotherly love, charity.*
>
> *For if these things are in you and abound, they shall not let you be idle nor unfruitful in the knowledge of our Lord Jesus Christ. But he that lacks these things is blind and walks feeling the way with his hand, having forgotten that he was purged from his old sins* (2 Peter 1:5-9).

This is a synthesis of what God wants to do in each one of our lives. He wants us to participate in His divine nature. God wants us to experience His feelings and His thoughts. Our own thoughts and feelings will betray us, but His thoughts and feelings will bless us and guide us to victory. He wants to live inside us and express Himself in and through us. He wants to give us the victory because He is the victory. We must be very careful when we claim God's promises that we have met His conditions. If we lack God's requirements, Peter says we will be blind and unable to remember being purged from our old sins. If we meet God's conditions, we will not be idle and unfruitful in our knowledge of Jesus Christ.

Tragically, as we look across the Christian church, especially the church in North America, it is very idle and unfruitful. (Not to mention blind and forgetful.) We have vast numbers of people calling themselves Christians who appear to be dozing when it is time to obey Jesus Christ. They are interested only in themselves and feeling good. They attempt to use God about His blood we are also talking about His death. This is a term that encompasses both the life and death of Jesus Christ.

> *For the soul (or life) of the flesh is in the blood, and I*
> *have given it to you to reconcile your persons (or souls)*
> *upon the altar; therefore the same blood reconciles the*
> *person* (Leviticus 17:11).

When we talk of putting the blood of Christ over us or being covered with the blood of Christ, we are talking about being dead to sin and allowing the resurrection life of Christ to live inside us to lead us, guide us, and empower us to live a victorious Christian life. We have taken Christ's blood and turned it into a code word for something magical that we throw out and sound holy while continuing to do our own thing, be our own god and go our own way. This is not what God has in mind.

> *This then is the promise which we have heard of him*
> *and declare unto you, That God is light, and in him is*
> *no darkness at all. If we say we have fellowship with him*
> *and walk in darkness, we lie, and do not the truth; but if*
> *we walk in the light, as he is in the light, we have commu-*
> *nion with him in the midst of us, and the blood of Jesus*
> *Christ, his Son cleanses us from all sin* (I John 1:5-7).

When offering a sacrifice in the Old Testament, the person had to put his hand on the animal before it was killed, before its blood was shed, and with an attitude of repentance recognize, "I deserve to die. This ought to be me. This is my death. I do not want to ever commit this sin again."

This was the difference between David and Saul. When Nathan the prophet went to David and told him about his sin, David did not say, "I am the king. I can decide. Who me? No, I have done nothing wrong." He did not try to justify or excuse it. He said, "I have sinned." He rent his garments and fell on his face before the Lord. He asked the Lord to cleanse him and make him whole, and the Lord did.

There were consequences and chastisement for the sin. Ugly incidents regarding his sons were probably spawned by David being involved in murder. The prophet said that bloodshed would not leave his house. But God restored King David and left him on the throne of Israel.

God kept His promises to David that one day one of his descendants would be the Savior and Messiah. He did not sideline David, and neither will He sideline any of us for our failures if we have an open heart before Him. When He points out our inadequacies, mistakes and sin, we need to be willing to repent and ask forgiveness saying, "I don't want to do it again. I want to set it right. I want Jesus to shine the light of His Holy Spirit into the shadows of my heart that I might be cleansed and made whole."

But if we say, "Who me?", and try to justify ourselves, we might go the route of King Saul. God can lift the anointing of His Holy Spirit if we continue headstrong along our own way, and we might not even know when He left.

Peter says we need to be giving all diligence to show forth in our faith, virtue; and in virtue, knowledge; and in knowledge, temperance . . . Notice the part about "giving all diligence." Another lie has been planted in the church which says that since our salvation is not by works, we do not have to do anything: It is a free gift of God. Then they say, "When is the free gift yours? When you receive it." All of a sudden they are talking about receiving an "it" instead of a "Him." The "it" is not going to save us; only the "Him" can save us. Only He can do those things which we cannot do for ourselves.

This is another definition of God's grace and His power, and they are not "magical" either. If we do not put our will into it and give all diligence to following Him by setting our heart on going His way, we will become idle and unfruitful in our knowledge of Jesus Christ. To become a victorious Christian takes everything we can put into it, and even that is not enough because we need Him, His grace, and His power. We need to learn to rest in and rely on the Lord, but nowhere does God say we are not to put our very best into trying to become what He wants us to be. Nowhere does the Bible say that we are called to mediocrity, to just do the least that we can to get by. My father told me, "Make no mistake, believing doctrines cannot save us even if they are true: only Jesus Christ can save us. We must believe Him."

The complete and unshakable assurance of salvation that we have comes only from submitting to His Lordship. If we will not submit to His authority over us, how is He supposed to discipline us when we need it, or control all our life's circumstances to mold us and make us into what He wants us to be? How is He supposed to protect us? How is He supposed to deliver us if we have retained areas of bondage to the enemy where we do not want His intervention? How is He supposed to keep us from being defeated by the enemy if we insist on leaving ourselves wide open to attack?

In order to be able to stand, in order to become what God wants us to be, and in order to have security for the future, we must submit to His authority and allow Him to be sovereign in our lives. We must remember that God is a gentleman in that He will not force Himself on us. We do not have to make ourselves perfect or clean ourselves up to come to God. He is willing to receive us, no matter what kind of problems we have. But we need to get one basic thing straight: who is the boss? Who has the last word? Are we willing to let Him intervene unconditionally in our affairs?

If you go into the hospital for surgery, you fill out and sign forms authorizing the doctor to take any measures he needs to take in order to save your life. If he opens you up and finds something else wrong (other than your original problem that you sought the doctor for), he is authorized to fix that too. Several times when I have been in the hospital, I have had to sign forms that authorize the hospital and the doctor. Once when I did not sign the forms, the hospital refused to treat me. The Lord is this way too. We cannot say, "I'm only going to let You do this much and no more." He might not operate. We might not see His power. We will not experience the fullness of the true anointing of His Holy Spirit if we try to limit Him in our lives.

You cannot just designate how much you want. You cannot come to Him and say, "Just solve this problem and no more." You must be willing to say, "Lord, here I am, and whatever needs to be fixed, You fix it. I will cooperate with You giving all diligence."

That is the prescription for being able to claim this promise: *For doing these things, ye shall never fall.* What things? *giving all diligence to the same, show forth virtue in your faith; and in virtue, knowledge; and in knowledge, temperance; and in temperance, patience; and in patience, fear of God; and in fear of God, brotherly love; and in brotherly love, charity.* Not only will we never fall, God promises that we will not be idle or unfruitful in the knowledge of our Lord Jesus Christ.

There is a big difference between obedience to the law (dead works of the flesh) and the obedience of faith (victorious life in the Spirit). In obedience to the law, we are trying to obey with our own resources. In the obedience of faith we put faith in Jesus Christ to give us the power (grace through His Holy Spirit) to carry out His will.

I would like you to consider whether you are idle or unfruitful in your knowledge of our Lord Jesus Christ. Would you like to be more effective and more fruitful, or do you think that you are effective and fruitful enough? Spend some time alone with the Lord, listening to Him and going over every area of your life, every relationship in your family, with your friends, and even with your enemies. Ask Him to show you where He wants you to be more effective and fruitful for Him. Ask Him to show you how to live the Beatitudes. Ask Him to plant His Beatitudes deep down in your heart.

If the Beatitudes are only in your mind, when you face an enemy ambush, you won't have time to dig them out and figure out how to apply them. That will not work. They must be planted deep in your heart so they will automatically flow out of your innermost being when you are under attack. This will happen only through practice, through going through crisis after crisis and evaluating your behavior afterwards with the Lord. You need to ask Him, "How did I do? What would You like to change? How can I do better next time?"

LET US PRAY:

*Lord, King Solomon built a glorious temple out of the spoils of battle, out of the booty that King David, his father, took away from Your enemies. Lord, I pray that we also will be able to take things away from the enemy who has bound and held hostage vast resources of millions, even billions of people that he has captive in man-made systems of confusion. Lord, may we understand the way Your kingdom works and operates so we will not just run around and do good things our own way, but be willing to do Your things Your way. May we allow You to come in and circumcise our hearts and with your two-edged sword, cut the control of our fleshly sinful nature; and then with Your fiery finger, write Your commandments on the tablets of our hearts and in our minds. Allow us to participate in*

*Your nature so that Your feelings and Your thoughts might dominate every aspect of our being, and You will live in us and be our God and we will be Your people, living in intimate communion and fellowship with You. May Your presence and peace shine forth out of us and affect all those with whom we come into contact. Amen.*

*All this, said David, the LORD made me understand in writing by his hand upon me, even all the works of this pattern.*

*And David said to Solomon, his son, Be strong and of good courage, and do it; fear not, nor be dismayed, for the LORD God, even my God, will be with thee; he will not leave thee, nor forsake thee, until thou hast finished all the work of the service of the house of the LORD (1 Chronicles 28:19-20).*

*And the LORD magnified Solomon exceedingly in the sight of all Israel and bestowed upon him such glory of the kingdom as had not been on any king before him in Israel (1 Chronicles 29:25).*

A very tragic thing happened in the book of Chronicles. We read how King David, as he was on his death bed, gave his last words and requests to his son Solomon. At that point in time, Israel was at its zenith morally and spiritually and was receiving the blessing of the Lord. The Lord had chosen Solomon to build the temple, and the first book of Chronicles ends with the children of Israel joyfully giving all of their gold and silver and precious stones (of their own free will) for the building of the temple. King David gave all of his personal wealth, and Chronicles records great rejoicing at the thought of building the temple of the Lord.

The second book of Chronicles starts with the glorious construction and dedication of Solomon's temple which ushered in the golden age of Israel, but this book has one of the most tragic endings in Scripture:

> *Moreover, all the princes of the priests and the people increased the rebellion, rebelling according to all the abominations of the Gentiles and polluting the house of the LORD which he had sanctified in Jerusalem.*
>
> *And the LORD God of their fathers sent to them by the hand of his messengers, rising up early, and sending because he had compassion on his people and on his dwelling place. But they mocked the messengers of God and despised his words and misused his prophets until the wrath of the LORD arose against his people, and there was no remedy.*
>
> *Therefore, he brought upon them the king of the Chaldees, who slew their young men with the sword in the house of their sanctuary and had no compassion upon young man or maiden, old man, or him that stooped for age; he gave them all into his hands.*
>
> *Likewise, all the vessels of the house of God, great and small, and the treasures of the house of the LORD and the treasures of the king and of his princes; all these he brought to Babylon.*
>
> *And they burnt the house of God and broke down the wall of Jerusalem and burnt all its palaces with fire and destroyed all its desirable vessels* (2 Chronicles 36:14-19).

What a tragic ending. What a terrible thing to happen to God's people and His sanctuary, His temple. Everything was demolished. All because God's people became unfaithful. Even though they continued their sacrifices and religious practices; even though they went through the motions of worshiping God and felt self-righteous, they didn't do the will of God.

They didn't listen to what God was telling them through His prophets. They didn't really grasp what He wanted when He said that to obey is better than sacrifice.

The temple was in ruins; the walls of Jerusalem were destroyed due to the disobedience and rebellion of God's people. But God did not leave things in this terrible state of disarray. He raised up a remnant under Ezra to rebuild the temple, and then He raised up Nehemiah to rally the people of God and rebuild the walls of Jerusalem. We are also living in a time when the (spiritual) temple of God needs to be restored, and the (spiritual) walls of God's protection around His people need to be rebuilt. The prophet Isaiah speaks about this:

*And shall say, Clear away, clear away, level the way, take away the stumblingblocks out of the way of my people.*

*For thus has said the high and lofty One that inhabits eternity, whose name is the Holy One;*

*I dwell in the high place and in holiness and with him also that is of a contrite and humble spirit to cause the spirit of the humble to live and to cause the heart of the contrite ones to live. For I will not contend for ever, neither will I be always be wroth: for by me is the spirit covered by the body, and I have made the souls. For the iniquity of his covetousness I was wroth and smote him: I hid my face and was wroth, and he went on rebelliously in the way of his heart. I have seen his ways and will heal him: I will lead him also and restore comforts unto him and to his mourners.*

*I create the fruit of the lips; Peace, peace to him that is far off and to him that is near, said the LORD; and healed him. But the wicked are like the sea in tempest, that can-*

*not rest, whose waters cast up mire and dirt. There is no
peace, saith my God, for the wicked* (Isaiah 57:14-21).

*Clear away, clear away, level the way, take away the stumblingblocks out of the way of My people.* This is what God wants
to do for each of us as individuals and collectively as a body. It
is much easier for God to work with individuals, than to collectively raise up an entire body that will walk in the way that
He wants them to walk. It is even harder, if not impossible, to
obtain the perfect cooperation of different church orders or
denominations. But certain enemy strongholds can only be
taken down when God mobilizes his entire army as a group.

*Remove the stumblingblocks out of the way of My people.*
That is what He is doing right now. God is in the business of
removing all stumblingblocks out of the way of His people. If
we are willing, God will remove the obstacles in our way that
prevent us from becoming effective and fruitful in His kingdom. On the other hand, some have put themselves in gilded
cages of their own making or their particular denomination or
group, and love having it so. The Lord wants to do away with
this. He will start shaking and rattling the cages until they all
come apart. He wants to break the yokes of bondage that have
enslaved His people for so long.

Isaiah 58 is one my favorite chapters in the Bible. Listen
to this.

> *Cry aloud, do not hold back; lift up thy voice like a shofar and preach to my people their rebellion and to the
> house of Jacob their sin* (Isaiah 58:1).

Whenever Israel turned away from God, He slipped in these
references to "Jacob," instead of calling them Israel. Jacob means
"conniver" or "supplanter." That is what God's people like to
do. We like to connive. We like to think, "What is the least I
can do and still be saved? What is the least I can do and still

have God's blessing? What is the least amount I can give and still have God bless me financially? What is the least amount of time I can give and still count on God to help me when I need Him? What is the least amount of service I can do in my church and still feel that I can call on the leadership in case I need help sometime?"

The natural man goes about things in this way. God wants to turn this around and declare to His people their rebellion. The Bible says that rebellion is the sin of witchcraft and to break the Word of the LORD is iniquity and idolatry (1 Samuel 15:23). We may think it is not serious to be rebellious and break the Word of the Lord, but they are two of the worst sins we could possibly imagine because they affect our relationship with God and bring us under bondage to the enemy.

> *That they seek me daily and want to know my ways, as people that do righteousness and have not forsaken the rights of their God: they ask me of the rights of righteousness and desire to approach God. Why have we fasted, they say, and thou dost not see? why have we afflicted our soul, and thou dost take no knowledge?* (Isaiah 58:2-3).

Our worship is different today, but we could say, "Why do we come to church, Lord? You haven't healed our land. We paid our tithe, Lord, yet our country is still running downhill." We have gone through the motions of worshiping God, but the thought that comes to my mind looking across North America is that what ought to be the fortress and city of God has become the city of organized religion. Instead of building the kingdom of God, we have built incredible religious machinery, much of which stands in the way of God being able to bless us, deliver us, and heal our land.

We are all susceptible to this kind of deception. For example, on the family level, it is easier to use a set of rules and regulations to run our families with than to be sensitive to the Spirit of God and allow Him to be the true leader of our homes. Reflect on your household and life, and ask God to show you if there are yokes of bondage that you have created that may have stifled the Lordship of Jesus Christ and the anointing of the Holy Spirit in your home to the point that Satan has been able to wreak havoc with your family. Many times, as a prerequisite to going forward to victory, we must be willing to dismantle those things we have created that God does not like. In the corporate structures of our churches, we need to do the same thing. We need to go over all the traditional structures that we have put into place and see if they are truly pleasing to the Lord, making sure there are no yokes of bondage that have been created by human effort that could be holding back the blessing of the Lord.

> *Why have we fasted, they say, and thou dost not see? why have we afflicted our soul, and thou dost take no knowledge? Behold in the day of your fast ye find your own pleasure and exact your own estates. Behold, ye fast for strife and debate, and to smite with the fist of wickedness: ye shall not fast as ye do this day to make your voice to be heard on high* (Isaiah 58:3-4).

Many churches (and families) end in splits today. People take off and go different ways. Finding new friends is easier than to reconciling the conflict. Quarrelling and strife are rampant in our families and businesses. If we are inclined to acknowledge the Lordship and authority of Jesus Christ, allowing Him to clean and purify our hearts to make us effective for Jesus Christ, Satan will attack. He will always probe our personal relationships first.

When personal relationships start going haywire, Satan

actually uses the man-made machinery that is in place to accelerate the conflict. "Well, you broke the rule that we made. You didn't treat me the way I treated you. You weren't supposed to do that, and you did it anyway." On and on and on. He tries to bring our relationships to an intellectual level of rules and regulations of who did what when, and who said what where, and who hurt whom how, instead of the heart to heart flow of the river of life relationships originating in the heart of God.

> *Behold, ye fast for strife and debate, and to smite with the fist of wickedness: ye shall not fast as ye do this day to make your voice to be heard on high. Is it such a fast that I have chosen? a day for a man to afflict his soul? is it to bow down his head as a bulrush, and to spread sackcloth and ashes under him? wilt thou call this a fast and an acceptable day to the LORD?* (Isaiah 58:4-5).

For many people that is what going to church is like. It is an obligation, something they force themselves to do in the hope that God will recognize and honor their sacrifice of choosing to go to church, rather than fishing or something else.

This is not what God wants. If you are still practicing your religion because you feel an obligation, and it is a great sacrifice for you, then you are in the same boat with the Jew who fasted in sackcloth and ashes to appease God. That is the wrong motivation. God wants a change of heart. He hopes to place joy in our hearts: a joy to be with our brothers and sisters in Christ, worshipping and fellowshipping with Him.

This is what makes difficult parenting. A certain amount of discipline is required to establish our children according to divine order. But if a rule is only reason our kids go to church, the day will come when they are on their own, and they may not go at all. Or they may go the rest of their lives out of a wrong motive and never attain all that God wants for them. If the parents are not filled with the joy, blessing and anointing of the Lord, it is very difficult for the children to be so filled.

> *Is not rather the fast that I have chosen, to loose the bands of wickedness, to undo the ties of oppression, to release into freedom those who are broken, and that ye break every yoke?* (Isaiah 58:6).

As Christians, we must be sure in our families and in our corporate expression of Christianity, that we are not legalistic, making heavier yokes and more chains for everyone. That is our human, natural way of doing things. When there is a problem or an abuse, we make more rules to ensure it doesn't happen again and put everyone in a strait jacket removing more liberty from the Holy Spirit. God intended for the Jews to be a people who would live in freedom with liberty to express themselves to Him, to worship and honor Him. Over the centuries, they added to the books of Moses and concocted an incredible number of rules and regulations.

By the time Jesus came, nobody could do anything without breaking a rule. They would meticulously keep these rules and think they were serving God, yet the blessing of God had left them long ago. Their rule-keeping was so extreme that when Jesus Christ walked among them, healed the blind, raised the dead, and did miracles they had never imagined, they did not give glory to God because Jesus was not interested in all their petty rules and regulations. He had come to share the heart of God with them, and they rejected it because it was foreign to the gilded cage of legalism they had surrounded themselves with.

We must be continually on our guard so the same thing does not happen to us. We need to look for chains and yokes, making sure we are not creating bondages. We cannot be saying, "Well, since this happened to me, and I had this negative experience, I had better make sure there is no way anyone else can get hurt by this. Therefore, we will have this and that rule," and thereby, we add to the Word of God. At the end of the Bible in the book of Revelation, there is a terrible curse on anyone who would add to or take away from the Word of God.

Obviously, we need order. Our churches and families are not to be totally uncontrolled. But we must have divine order, God-ordained order, and not some other order we devised as a substitute for God's order. We must be sure to shoulder our God-ordained responsibilities. If you are the head of the household, your responsibility is to guarantee that your household is run according to God's order, not according to rules you made up or learned somewhere. Likewise, if you are part of the leadership of a church, it is your responsibility to be participating in God's order and not some other kind of order.

> Is it not to share thy bread with the hungry and that thou bring the poor that are cast out into thy house? when thou seest the naked, that thou cover him; and that thou not hide thyself from thy brother? Then shall thy light break forth as the morning, and thine health shall spring forth speedily: and thy righteousness shall go before thee; the glory of the LORD shall gather thee. Then shalt thou call, and thou shalt hear the LORD; thou shalt cry, and he shall say, Here I am. If thou take away from the midst of thee the yoke, the putting forth of the finger, and speaking vanity (Isaiah 58:7-9).

As I travel across this continent, I hear many prayers in churches, and most people want great things from God. "Lord, heal our land. Lord, heal me when I'm sick. Lord, we don't have enough money. Lord, save our schools." Rarely do I see spectacular, clear-cut answers to prayer where the power of God has descended and there is a distinct difference between those who are serving God and those who are not. If God's conditions have not been met by those who claim to belong to Him, we have not allowed the Lord to work in and through us.

*...to share thy bread with the hungry and that thou bring the poor that are cast out to thy house.* One time when we were very poor, growing up on a missionary base, my Dad started to apply some of these promises and meet some of the conditions. He had a whole book of all of the promises in Scripture. He would get down on his knees and ask the Lord what He wanted him to do to meet some of these conditions and activate God's promises. Dad did some "strange" things for which he was severely criticized.

One occurred when we were to host a big banquet for the government dignitaries who were in charge of the Ministry of Government. The missionaries were about to be kicked out of the country, so the mission wanted to give the leaders of the government a favorable impression of the mission base. An airplane was sent to fly the dignitaries from the capital city to the missionary compound. Buying food and supplies for a special banquet drained the mission public relations fund. Everyone got out their best lace tablecloths and china. The banquet centered at our house because my dad was in charge of the technical work for the mission. It was his job to handle the government dignitaries. My mom and some of the ladies who were the best cooks among the missionary wives prepared a special dinner. We took our living room furniture out and put extra tables in our living room and dining room. But then the Director of our mission called with a report that there was bad weather, and the trip had been canceled and put off a week. So there we were with this exquisite banquet and no invited guests. The Director wanted to know if our family could eat all the food and then pay the public relations fund back.

Dad and Ricardo had just been reading in their Bibles where it said that if the wedding guests who had been invited did not come, you were to go out into the highways and byways and compel them to come in. Ricardo felt that this was what we should do. There were a lot of poor neighbors outside the gates of the mission compound. We were not supposed to be working with them because we had only been chartered to work with Indians, and many of our missionary coworkers feared that if we worked with these needy Spanish speakers, we would jeopardize our government contract. So we had been sitting there allowing horrendous need to occur right at our very gate. Dad informed the Director that in regard to the banquet, we were going to do what the Bible said and round up all the poor, hungry neighbors and feed them.

Then Dad went out with the mission vehicles and loaded up the poor people and brought them to our house where he sat them down at the tables with the lace tablecloths and the fine china, and we served them the banquet.

I can still remember serving at that banquet when a little old guy (I have never seen before or since) came hobbling up the hill to ask if we could give him a drink of water. He was minus one leg, hobbling around on crutches, sporting a long white beard and long white hair. He looked strange, and wore strange clothes. My dad said, "Sure! In fact we can give you a whole banquet." He took him in and sat him at the head of one of the tables. We gave him a place to stay, and he pronounced a blessing on us before he left the next day. We never saw him again. Even as a kid, I knew that it said somewhere in my Bible that some have entertained angels unawares.

Some of the missionaries became very glad and joyful over what had happened. But others became very hard and bitter and formed a committee to insist that my dad should pay for all this personally because the public relations fund was about to go in the red. They wanted to know how they were going to pay for the real banquet next week when all the invited dignitaries were coming?

The next week the hostile government officials arrived. We showed them around, put on presentations of what we were doing, and fed them another banquet (this time it was pot luck). Since the PR fund was empty, each missionary family made a dish and sent it over to our house. Miraculously, these men, who had come with their minds already made up to remove our mission from their country went home and decided not to cancel the mission contract after all. God had touched their hearts. I am convinced that the real spiritual battle was won the week before when we served the first banquet to our poor neighbors.

> *Then said he (Jesus) also to him that invited him,*
> *When thou makest a dinner or a supper, call not thy*
> *friends nor thy brethren neither thy kinsmen nor thy*
> *rich neighbours, lest they also invite thee again, and*
> *a recompense be made thee. But when thou makest a*
> *banquet, call the poor, the maimed, the lame, the blind,*
> *and thou shalt be blessed* (Luke 14:12-14).

A few weeks later, God moved among these poor neighbors who lived outside the gate of the mission compound. They formed a little church and got jobs harvesting rice by hand out in the fields, making very little. The rice crop was lost that year so they did not get any money, and they were starving. Dad decided that whoever came to our door would not be turned away, and if they asked for food, we would share what we had; if they asked for money, we would give each person twenty pesos (equivalent to about five dollars today).

We never knew how much money would come in each month because we were living by faith. We always knew that at the end of the month we would get the bills and the check from the mission office, and most of the time they matched. But sometimes we were in the red. Dad would give out more money in that month helping people than we normally received in an entire month. But more needy cases kept coming, and he prayed about each one and believed the Lord would lay on his heart how much to give them or what to give them from our house.

Some of our fellow missionaries told Dad that the people were going to take advantage of him, and he would never be able to stop it; others brought twenty pesos bills of their own over to my parents to help with this endeavor. Dozens of people were helped, and not a one came back to ask for money a second time. When we got our monthly check, it was for the amount we normally received, plus the sum of all the money that Dad had given away.

Several days later, a woman came to our house and tried to pawn her watch to my mother. She explained that she needed money to buy some presentable clothes for her husband (his were torn and stained work clothes) so she could take him to church (he was too ashamed to go in his work clothes). My mother didn't want to take this poor lady's watch so she suggested that they pray about the situation. A few minutes later, one of my mom's missionary friends came over with a whole armload of clothes that her son had outgrown. They were the exact size that the lady was looking for, and she was able to take her husband, Miro, to church that very night. He had a glorious encounter with the Lord, and a revival was sparked among the poor people.

Then these poor Christians found a sick man with tuberculosis who was worse off than they were, and they began helping him. No one knew it was tuberculosis, but he was very sick and wasted away. My dad used the mission jeep and drove the guy to the clinic inside our mission compound. The doctor took one look at him and said, "Chad, you've got to get this guy out of here. He's got tuberculosis. If you leave him here he could infect other people. I don't care what you do, but get rid of him."

Dad said, "You mean you're not going to put him in a hospital bed? You're not going to take care of him?"

"No! We can't have this infection around. Get him out of here. Take him back where you found him." Dad told him where he found him, and the doctor said, "Don't take him back there either. He'll infect all those people too, and we'll have an epidemic of tuberculosis on our hands. Send him back to his home to die."

Dad pled with the doctor and some of the other missionaries, but no one would budge. As Dad drove away with this sick fellow in the jeep (knowing in his heart that this was not the way the Lord Jesus would have handled this situation), he tried to explain to Miro, the new convert, who had nothing, the position of the mission. He also told him about the danger to Miro, his wife and children to be around this guy.

Miro said, "We can't do that. If he can't stay in your clinic, he can continue to stay in my home. In fact, I'll give him my bed."

When they arrived at Miro's home, Dad was still saying, "But Miro, you don't understand. This guy has tuberculosis, and your home has enough hygiene problems as it is. Show me your bed."

Miro's bed was a gunnysack in the corner on the dirt floor of the little hut he lived in. That was what he was going to give this man who was worse off than he was. Miro was going to sleep on the bare ground. As Dad was leaving Miro's house, Miro looked at him and said, "My brother died of tuberculosis, and I know exactly what I'm getting into." Miro was confused because what the missionaries were doing did not seem to line up with what he was reading in the Word of God.

My Dad gathered the little congregation of poor believers together, and they prayed for the sick fellow. Then they took up a collection for him, and there was just enough money to send him to the government TB sanitarium in the state capital. The sick man had a twelve year old son with him who was well. The two of them were sent down the line on the bus, but halfway to the TB hospital, the Lord healed the fellow. He told his son that he knew he was well, but they continued to the sanitarium where the government doctors took chest x-rays and found no signs of tuberculosis. The next day, they arrived back at our mission compound, and my dad did not even recognize the man until he identified himself. He was in perfect heath.

> *Is it not to share thy bread with the hungry and that thou bring the poor that are cast out to thy house? when thou seest the naked, that thou cover him; and that thou not hide thyself from thy brother?* (Isaiah 58:7).

My wife, Marina, is the middle child out of a more or less typical Colombian family of nine children. We have many relatives. We went through a time when it was one thing after another with her family. We would help one, and then another would be in dire need. One time a business they owned went under, and at once four of them were out of work. In Colombia, there is no safety net. There is no social security, or unemployment benefits. If the family will not help someone in need, they can literally starve to death. Sometimes it requires great sacrifice.

As the Lord has impressed this verse on us, it has been amazing to look back on the way He has provided. When the four of them were out of work, we prayed. The Lord showed us ways to help three of them. But the only thing we could do for the fourth was to trade our car for a taxi which he could drive to support his family and help support my mother-in-law. We had been two years without a car in Colombia, and finally, the Lord had provided one. I felt in my heart we should do it, as did my wife, but she knew that if we did, we would be without a car which we needed for the ministry. It was not an easy choice.

Finally, one night I said, "It comes down to this: are we going to help your family or not? If we are, we had better do it." So we did. The answer of the Lord was almost immediate. We turned the car over to the dealer in the morning, and by evening the Lord had provided a car for us that was three times better than the one we gave away. We did not know this would happen when we gave ours away, but the Lord was very good to us.

*Then shall thy light break forth as the morning, and thine health shall spring forth speedily: and thy righteousness shall go before thee.*

Remember that righteousness also means acts of justice, or doing, as well as being the kind of people God wants us to be. Because we are being the kind of people God wants us to be, we will be doing the kind of things God wants us to do.

*And thy righteousness shall go before thee; the glory of the LORD shall gather thee.*

We do not even have to defend ourselves from being attacked from behind. God will be watching our backs. The Lord will be protecting us.

*Then shalt thou call, and thou shalt hear the LORD; thou shalt cry, and he shall say, Here I am. If thou take away from the midst of thee the yoke, the putting forth of the finger, and speaking vanity; and if thou pour out thy soul to the hungry, and satisfy the afflicted soul; then shall thy light rise in obscurity, and thy darkness be as the noonday:* (Isaiah 58:9-10).

If our night is going to become like the noonday, imagine what the noonday will be like? We do not have any idea of the things that God wants to do for us, in us, and through us. Most of us use only a fraction of the grace that God has for us. We never get past making the initial sacrifices involved with giving up our own way. We never get to where our light breaks forth like the dawn, our healing appears, our righteousness goes before us, the glory of the Lord gathers us, and when we call, the Lord answers, *Here am I.*

*If thou take away from the midst of thee the yoke...* It is important to make sure we are not putting yokes of oppression on other people. If we need to deal with a problem in someone's life, we must do it out of a heart filled with mercy and love. We must not point the finger. But for the grace of God that could be us. We must put ourselves in that person's place and do as we would have them do to us.

> *If thou pour out thy soul to the hungry, and satisfy the afflicted soul; then shall thy light rise in obscurity, and thy darkness be as the noonday: and the LORD shall guide thee continually.*

Sometimes? Every once in a while? It says the Lord will guide you continually. Can you look at your life and say that the Lord guides you continually? Whenever you cry to the Lord does He say, *Here I am?*

> *...and satisfy thy soul in drought, and make fat thy bones; and thou shalt be like a watered garden.*

If we are truly servants of the Lord, in the middle of a raging spiritual conflict, this is not the time for opulence. The Lord has promised to satisfy our needs. Every time He gives us beyond what we need, I believe we should use it for His honor and glory to satisfy the needs of others or to see His work go forward as He would lay on our hearts. We need to get back to our needs, not our wants.

Many times God has blessed me with better things than I thought I needed, but that is up to Him. I believe I should look to Him and ask Him for what I need for the job He has called me to do. When my needs are being met, I should not come up with a personal wish list, spending money on goodies to gratify myself rather than on ammunition to fight the enemy. If you were a soldier in a foxhole, running low on ammunition, what would you want? A load of ice cream or a load of ammunition? Would you rather have a feather bed or what you needed to face the enemy? This is the bottom line. Jesus said: *But seek ye first the kingdom of God and his righteousness, and all these things shall be added unto you* (Matthew 6:33).

Satan is the prince of this world and controls most of the worldly resources. Think of what could be done if even a few of us were willing to release God in our lives through what we have. What if we were willing to look to Him only for what we need, instead of for what we want? What if we were willing to ask Him to show us what He wants us to do with our resources? We could begin a dynamic of blessing. God really does want to bless us. There is prosperity in Jesus Christ, but it is not a selfish prosperity. God wants to prosper us so we can reveal God the Father to those in the world who cannot see Him, and they might see our good works and praise our Father in heaven.

In the Sermon on the Mount, Jesus talks about us being the salt of the earth and the light of the world. We are a city set on a hill that cannot be hidden. Then He says, *Let your light so shine before men that they may see your good works and glorify your Father who is in the heavens.* This is what God wants. We cannot just preach about Jesus Christ and never physically help someone, or the world will not be able to see God the Father. Some churches preach about Christ, but never help anyone, and other churches do many good works, but never tell anyone why. Some churches are preaching and teaching without the anointing of the Holy Spirit to help things go smoothly. God wants everything in its proper place.

I have found that many Christians are victims of a very subtle error (a reordering of truth) that has crept into Christendom and goes something like this: 1) The first step in your Christian life is to accept Jesus as your Savior. 2) At a later date in your Christian walk, you may experience a second work of grace as Christ anoints you with his Holy Spirit (This is referred to by some as sanctification and by others as "the baptism in the Holy Spirit." 3) For an elite and special group of saints, there remains an optional third step of making Jesus Christ the Lord of their lives. This is normally done only by those who are called into missionary service, the clergy, or some type of specialized ministry.

The truth needs to be applied to our practical Christian lives as follows: 1) As the basis of Christian faith, we must receive Jesus Christ who is our Lord and Savior. We must surrender to His authority from the start and renounce our own way (and the ways of the world) so we might go His way. 2) By grace He will send us the Comforter (Holy Spirit) to lead us into all truth and to clothe us (equip us) with the very character and power of God (2 Peter Chapter 1). The Holy Spirit will cleanse and purify our hearts so we might 3) Enter into a right relationship with God the Father.

Only the pure in heart will see God (the Father). It is only through a right relationship with the Father that we will ever be able to live a victorious Christian life and win the battle against the hosts of darkness. These are the sons of God (the Father) who are joint-heirs with Jesus Christ, projecting the peace of the Father into a lost and dying world. These are those who will inspire hope to those who live in darkness.

Look at what will happen:

> *And the LORD shall guide thee continually, and satisfy thy soul in drought, and make fat thy bones: and thou*

*shalt be like a watered garden, and like a spring of water, whose waters do not fail* (Isaiah 58:11).

Those around us will look at us, and will want to be like us, and will have hope. They will want to have what we have, the peace and joy of knowing God. They will want to be able to help others the way we are helping others. They will look at us and say, "Yes, these people are doing what is right. This is real righteousness. This is justice. I wish I could be like that." Jesus wants those in the world to be able to look at our good works (of faith) and praise our Father in heaven, instead of saying, "I don't want to be like that bunch of crazy fanatics over there. Wild horses couldn't drag me into that kooky place." If we do not present hope to the world, and if they cannot see God in us, they will not want to listen to us when we attempt to share the gospel with them.

Then Isaiah says:

*And they shall build up out of thee the old waste places: thou shalt raise up the fallen foundations of many generations; and thou shalt be called, The repairer of the breach, The restorer of paths to dwell in* (Isaiah 58:12).

Often what God really wanted is in ruins. The church started in the upper room, but after a few centuries, it was off into left field. Every now and then a genuine revival would start in the right direction, but over the long history of the church, each one of these moves of God ended up being institutionalized or denominationalized. Men put a yoke where God had meant freedom. They built a cage where God wanted His Holy Spirit to have liberty, and so they kept putting out the fire. God's plans for the church became ancient ruins like His plans for the children of Israel. But God wants to raise up the fallen foundations, and He wants to build up out of us the old waste places and reconstruct according to His original design.

*For no one can lay another foundation than that laid,*
*which is Jesus the Christ* (1 Corinthians 3:11).

That which is not built on obedience to Jesus Christ will not stand when the storm comes. Many impressive religious organizations have been built on the sand. If we wish to claim these glorious promises of God from this passage in Isaiah, we must raise up the fallen foundations.

*And I, if I be lifted up from the earth, will draw all men*
*unto me* (John 12:32).

*Thou shalt be called, The repairer of the breach.* The walls around the city were for defense from the enemy. The spiritual walls of God's protection around our families, our churches, and our society are now down and in ruins so the enemy is coming in like a flood. He is making off with our children; he has wrecked the educational system; he is in the universities and politics; he runs the economic system. No matter where we turn, it seems that Satan has infiltrated and is running rampant because the walls are in ruins. These are spiritual walls that God wanted to have around His people (church) to protect them. In fact, God's people, His church, are supposed to be these spiritual walls of defense that keep the enemy from destroying our society.

If we meet the conditions of this tremendous promise, God says we can rebuild, raise up, repair, and restore what God wanted. We can rebuild the old waste places of the true fortress of God; we can raise up the fallen foundations, raise up the Lord Jesus Christ as the Master of everyone and everything; we can repair the breach and stop the enemy onslaught on God's people; we can restore paths to dwell in and reconcile our families. The Lord promises that:

*So shall they fear the name of the LORD from the*
*west, and his glory from the rising of the sun; for he*

*shall come like a violent river impelled by the breath*
*(or Spirit) of the LORD. And the Redeemer shall come*
*to Zion and unto those that turn from the rebellion in*
*Jacob, said the LORD* (Isaiah 59:19-20).

We are getting closer and closer to the time when the Lord
Jesus will come back, and every man-made system of hypocrisy will come down. We are not talking about renewing man's
systems, but about looking to the Lord to redeem his people
and deliver them from the bondage of their own good ideas so
we might build His kingdom from now on according to His
plans instead of our own.

*Thou shalt be called, The repairer of the breach, The restorer*
*of paths to dwell in.* One of the things that God wants to restore
under His anointing and protection is our families. Families are
the basic building block of society and of the church. The church
will never be strong until it has strong families. Churches as a
collection of individuals can only go so far. Satan has attacked
the Christian family with all of his might. He has tried to destroy
our values, foment sexual perversion, open a generation gap,
promote abortion, and destroy Christian marriage. But before
you throw in the towel in the face of this onslaught, listen to
the promises of God.

*If thou turn away thy foot from the sabbath, from*
*doing thy will on my holy day; and call the sabbath the*
*delightful, holy, glorious day of the LORD; and shalt*
*honour him by not doing thine own ways, nor seeking*
*thine own will, nor speaking thine own words: then*
*shalt thou delight thyself in the LORD; and I will cause*
*thee to ride upon the high places of the earth and cause*
*thee to eat of the heritage of Jacob thy father: for the*
*mouth of the LORD has spoken it.* (Isaiah 58:13-14).

Remember that under the New Covenant, the Sabbath day,

which involves God's rest, is really for us every day. It is every day that God wants us to rest from being our own god, to rest from making our own decisions and from striving to go our own way. He wants us to rest in Him every day. He still wants us to take at least one day a week out for physical rest. But for us, every day should be a Sabbath day. We should enter into and live in the rest of the Lord, asking Him to lead us, guide us, fight our battles and go before us. We need to set our will to follow Him and do those things that He would have us to do.

LET US PRAY:

*Heavenly Father, I ask that You might make us into overcomers, individually and as a company. Lord, as we have turned from what we know to be wrong in our lives, and as we have gone over personal relationships that we know need improvement, I pray that You would save us from one of the greatest problems of all. Save us from those things that appear to be good, those things that we think are wonderful, and we are pleased and complacent with. But there are things in this category that may be an abomination before You. Things that we like, but that You do not like. Lord, I pray that You would work in our hearts. Purify our hearts until we can feel the same way that You do about all that is not right in us. May we not be deceived by the enemy who would deceive the very elect, if that were possible, into thinking that something is good and of You when that is really not the case.*

*Lord, I pray for sharp discernment. I ask for Your power and anointing to go forward. I ask that You would take your entire body and form it into a well-trained fighting unit that can go forward to victory and*

*can reach out to others and help them in Your name.*
*Help us stand and shine as a brilliant light that will*
*illuminate the path so those outside will be able to find*
*their way to you, and those in the world might see your*
*hope in us and be drawn to open their hearts to You.*
*May everything we do glorify you, Holy Father.*
*Amen.*

J esus public teaching ministry began with the proclamation
of the Beatitudes. It ended with the proclamation of seven
woes to the religious leaders of His day as they confirmed their
rejection of Jesus' message and ministry. After His triumphal
entry into Jerusalem on Palm Sunday, the people were ready to
make Jesus their king until He entered the temple and began
driving out the buyers and sellers. His decision to cleanse the
temple for the second time by overturning the tables of the
moneychangers precipitated a conflict with the chief priests,
scribes, Pharisees, and other leaders. If Jesus were truly going
to be King, he would need to dismantle all the corrupt religious
machinery that stood between the people and a right relationship with God. The din and chaos of the buyers and sellers was
drowning out true communication with God.

> ...and (he) said unto them, It is written, My house shall
> be called the house of prayer; but ye have made it a den
> of thieves (Matthew 21:13).

The people wanted Jesus as their King as long as He confined
His ministry to the working of miracles. They wanted to be
fed and healed, but they did not want radical surgery to their
religious way of life. Many felt carnally secure in their ability
to procure the proper offering or sacrifice with money at their
own convenience. These were the buyers that Jesus drove from
the temple. The sellers, represented by the religious leaders, were
even more dependent on this illicit economic activity in the
house of God because it was their primary source of income.

When Jesus interrupted their flow of cash right at Passover (the most profitable time of the year), they reacted desperately.

After several pointed parables by the Lord, these evil men tried to trap Jesus by asking Him difficult questions. They failed miserably, and the Scripture says:

*And no one was able to answer him a word, neither dared anyone from that day forth ask him any more questions.*

*Then Jesus spoke to the multitude and to his disciples, saying, The scribes and the Pharisees have sat down in Moses' seat; therefore, whatever they bid you to observe, observe it and do it, but do not act according to their works, for they say and do not do it.*

*For they bind burdens that are heavy and grievous to bear and lay them on men's shoulders, but they themselves will not move them with one of their fingers. But they do all their works that they may be seen of men: they make broad their phylacteries and enlarge the borders of their garments and love the first place at feasts and the chief seats in the synagogues and greetings in the markets and to be called of men, Rabbi, Rabbi.*

*But, as for you, desire not to be called Rabbi, for one is your Master, the Christ; and you are all brothers. And call no one your father upon the earth, for one is your Father, who is in the heavens. Neither be ye called masters, for one is your Master, the Christ. But he that is the greatest among you shall be your servant. And whosoever shall exalt himself shall be humbled, and he that shall humble himself shall be exalted* (Matthew 22:46-23:12),

Jesus then proclaimed the seven woes which correlate with the seven Beatitudes in Matthew, Chapter 5. With the proclamation of these woes, Jesus makes it clear that not only did the scribes and Pharisees reject Him and His message, they insisted on doing the exact opposite of what He proposed. Let us contrast these woes, one by one, with the Beatitudes.

The first woe:

> *But woe unto you, scribes and Pharisees, hypocrites! for ye shut up the kingdom of the heavens in front of men; for ye neither go in yourselves, neither suffer ye those that are entering to go in* (Matthew 23:13).

The first beatitude:

> *Blessed are the poor in spirit, for theirs is the kingdom of the heavens.*

Not only do these proud religious leaders refuse to enter the true kingdom of heaven, they stand in the way and prevent others from entering. When those outside observe these representatives of God, they see nothing but hypocrisy, avarice, and greed, causing many to reject the gospel. The church age is going to close with a time of extreme woe for those church leaders who refuse to enter the kingdom of God through the narrow gate and also prevent others from doing so. These are the ones who have only made a shallow, superficial commitment to God and teach others to do likewise. God cannot judge the world until He cleans up His church. Given the degree of selfishness and corruption rampant in the church today, many of those in the world can't be blamed for rejecting it.

The second woe:

> *Woe unto you, scribes and Pharisees, hypocrites! for ye compass sea and land to make one proselyte, and when he is made, ye make him twofold more a son of hell than yourselves* (Matthew 23:15).

The second beatitude:

*Blessed are those that mourn, for they shall be
comforted.*

Those who have chosen to follow Christ must leave behind
many things that are dear to them as they take up their cross
and follow Him. "Only he who loses his life for my sake and
the gospel will find it," says the Lord. The one who is dead in
Christ will experience the resurrection power of God that
raised Jesus from the dead; he will be comforted by receiving
the Comforter. The Comforter is nothing less than God's Holy
Spirit. Those who have the Holy Spirit are sealed by God and
operate in His authority. Those who mourn are sincere with
God. They are not hypocrites.

The comforted follow the still small voice of Jesus Christ,
and they win converts that follow Jesus Christ. The scribes and
Pharisees, on the other hand, win proselytes to their sect, order,
or denomination. The comforted pay attention to the ways of
the Lord and realize (like Moses) that how we implement the
kingdom of God (our modus operandi) is many times more
important than our plans and ambitions. The proselytes of the
scribes and Pharisees of religious humanism believe that the
end justifies the means. They think nothing of taking the law
into their own hands to implement their lofty plans and ambitions by using God's name.

The third woe:

*Woe unto you, ye blind guides, who say, Whosoever
shall swear by the temple, it is nothing; but whosoever
shall swear by the gold of the temple, he is a debtor!
Ye fools and blind, for which is greater, the gold or the
temple that sanctifies the gold? And, Whosoever shall
swear by the altar, it is nothing; but whosoever swears
by the gift that is upon it, he is a debtor. Ye fools and
blind, for which one is greater, the gift or the altar that*

*sanctifies the gift? Whosoever therefore shall swear by the altar, swears by it and by all things thereon. And whosoever shall swear by the temple, swears by it and by Him that dwells therein. And he that shall swear by the heaven, swears by the throne of God and by Him that sits thereon* (Matthew 23:16-22).

The third beatitude:

*Blessed are the meek, for they shall inherit the earth.*

The meek are those who submit every area of their existence to the Lordship of Jesus Christ. The hypocrite will do the opposite; he will interpret God's precepts according to his own understanding or according to the doctrine of his organization.

The scribes and Pharisees, as opposed to the meek, are busy trying to save their lives and their worldly treasures. Since they do not have the genuine Holy Spirit, they lack the authority of God in their dealings with others. For this reason, they invoke oaths and swear by the gold of the temple. But an oath by the temple is nothing to them, and an oath by the altar is nonbinding. They cannot tolerate the cost of putting everything on the altar and thereby becoming part of that great temple made without hands that God is raising up as His dwelling place.

In the Sermon on the Mount, Jesus tells us to not swear oaths by anything. We are to let our yes be yes and our no be no. Jesus says anything beyond this comes of evil. Jesus Christ must have complete authority over us if we are to be able to speak with His authority. Those unwilling to mourn over their own plans will never receive the Holy Spirit. Without the real Holy Spirit, they will never be able to be meek before the Lord. They will never speak with true authority from God. Therefore, they will fall into the trap of the devil and justify their actions with pious sounding oaths. At present, no one can swear an oath by the gold of the temple or by the gift on the altar because that was destroyed as a result of the fulfillment of Jesus' prophetic words of authority in this section of Scripture. It has been my experience in North America to hear many swear by the Bible and in South America to hear many swear by their mother (or by Jesus' mother) when they do not have true authority from God.

The meek are those who, moved by the Spirit of God, place all aspects of their existence under the authority of Jesus Christ. The blind guides do the opposite; they interpret the precepts of God according to their own criteria or according to the doctrine of their religious confession.

The fourth woe:

> Woe unto you, scribes and Pharisees, hypocrites! for ye pay tithe of mint and anise and cummin and have omitted that which is more important of the law: judgment, mercy, and faith; these were expedient for ye to have done, and not to leave the other undone. Ye blind guides, who strain at a gnat and swallow a camel (Matthew 23:23-24).

The fourth beatitude:

> Blessed are those who hunger and thirst for righteousness, for they shall be satisfied.

Righteousness is the manifestation of right judgment, mercy, and faith in our lives that occurs only when God's Holy Spirit dwells within us. Righteousness is composed of these two components: 1) Being (through grace) the person God wants us to be and 2) Doing (by faith) those acts of justice and mercy that God wants us to do. Righteousness is both being and doing right. This is what the religious legalists are never able to obtain, no matter how hard they try. They strive to tithe the mint, dill, and cumin (the smallest herbs in the garden), while they neglect the foundational virtues of the Christian faith. Being filled with the presence of God is the only way to rest and be satisfied. The legalist will never be satisfied, no matter how many good rules he tries to keep, or how many excellent Christian principles he tries to implement in his own strength.

The fifth woe:

> *Woe unto you, scribes and Pharisees, hypocrites! for ye make clean the outside of the cup or of the platter, but within they are full of extortion and incontinence. Thou blind Pharisee, cleanse first that which is within the cup and platter that the outside of them may be clean also* (Matthew 23:25-26).

The fifth beatitude:

> *Blessed are the merciful, for they shall obtain mercy.*

Showing mercy means treating others the way we would like to be treated, being willing to forgive and restore our brother (or even our enemy) who has wronged us. It is the sacrificial love of God flowing from a tender heart filled with compassion for those in need. Extortion and incontinence are the opposite of mercy. They take advantage of those in need. The religious hypocrite has an outwardly pious appearance, but is ready to pounce on and devour others whenever it is to his advantage to do so. There are many charitable ministries that live off the predicament of the poor people they are claiming to help.

The sixth woe:

> *Woe unto you, scribes and Pharisees, hypocrites! for ye are like unto whitewashed sepulchers, who indeed appear beautiful outside, but inside are full of dead men's bones and of all uncleanness. Even so ye also outwardly appear righteous unto men, but within ye are full of hypocrisy and iniquity* (Matthew 23:27-28).

The sixth beatitude:

> *Blessed are the pure in heart, for they shall see God.*

It takes a pure heart to see God. The heart is the mirror of our soul, created to reflect the image of God. If it is stained and defiled with hypocrisy and iniquity, it cannot reflect the image of God. This is what causes spiritual blindness. The reason Jesus called these seemingly respectable religious leaders blind guides is because their hearts were rotten to the core. Jesus says that if the blind lead the blind, both will fall into a pit (Luke 6:39).

The seventh woe:

*Woe unto you, scribes and Pharisees, hypocrites! because ye build the tombs of the prophets and adorn the sepulchers of the righteous and say, If we had been in the days of our fathers, we would not have been partakers with them in the blood of the prophets. Therefore ye are witnesses unto yourselves that ye are the sons of those who murdered the prophets. Fill ye up then the measure of your fathers. Ye serpents, ye generation of vipers, how can ye escape the judgment of hell?* (Matthew 23:29-33).

The seventh beatitude:

*Blessed are the peacemakers, for they shall be called the sons of God.*

Here we have the true sons of God on one hand and those who witness against themselves that they are the sons of those who murdered the prophets on the other. The pure hearts of the sons of God radiate peace (integrity). The rotten hearts of the hypocrites (which are full of extortion and incontinence) generate murder and violence toward those who would attempt to illuminate them with God's truth. (Bear in mind that Jesus equates harboring an angry grudge with murder in Matthew 5:21).

*Therefore, behold, I send unto you prophets and wise men and scribes, and some of them ye shall kill and crucify, and some of them ye shall scourge in your synagogues and persecute them from city to city, that upon you may come all the righteous blood shed upon the*

*earth from the blood of righteous Abel unto the blood
of Zacharias son of Barachias, whom ye murdered
between the temple and the altar. Verily I say unto you,
All these things shall come upon this generation.*

*O Jerusalem, Jerusalem, thou that didst kill the proph-
ets and stone those who are sent unto thee, how often
I desired to gather thy children together, even as a hen
gathers her chickens under her wings, and ye would
not! Behold, your house is left unto you desolate. For
I say unto you, Ye shall not see me from now on until
ye shall say, Blessed is he that comes in the name of the
Lord* (Matthew 23:34-39).

Compare the above Scripture to the continuation of the
remaining two beatitudes in Matthew Chapter 5.

*Blessed are those who suffer persecution for righteous-
ness' sake, for theirs is the kingdom of the heavens.*

*Blessed are ye when men shall revile you and persecute
you and shall say all manner of evil against you falsely
for my sake. Rejoice and be exceeding glad, for great is
your reward in the heavens; for so they persecuted the
prophets who were before you* (Matthew 5:10-12).

For the sons of God, persecution is the mark of true sonship.
But woe to those who are doing the persecution. The hypocrites
will always persecute the true sons of God. The religious traditions of men will always contradict the true revelation of God.
Prophets do not normally get into serious trouble until they
drive the buyers and sellers from the temple. When the buyers
are told they may bypass the temple vendors and go directly
to God the Father with their problems and concerns through
the mediation of the Lord Jesus Christ, when the sellers are
confronted for building their own kingdoms in the name of

the Lord and using the things of God to line their own pockets and exalt their own name (or the name of their organization) instead of God's name, when the existing religious machinery becomes threatened by the prophetic Word of the Lord, then watch out. This is when the generation of vipers will attack. They will attack whenever they are cornered and their kingdom is threatened. It has been said that those who attempt to do God's work man's way will always persecute those who do God's work God's way.

> *And Jesus went out and departed from the temple, and his disciples came to him to show him the buildings of the temple. And Jesus said unto them, See ye not all these things? verily I say unto you, There shall not be left here one stone upon another that shall not be thrown down.* (Matthew 24:1-2).

The Old Testament age ended with the complete destruction of the temple about AD 70. After the temple had been burned, Roman soldiers pried apart every stone seeking precious metals that had been melted in the fire and trickled down into the cracks. The whole apostate religious machinery that rejected the Lord was destroyed. Not one stone was left on top of another. Not one ounce of the temple gold that the Pharisees had sworn by was left. Even though almost everyone and everything in Jerusalem was destroyed, all the true Christians escaped unharmed. In the confusion surrounding the Roman siege of Jerusalem, two opposing factions of Jews had a bloody fight for control of the temple citadel. The Christians took this as the sign given by the Lord and fled (the abomination of desolation spoken of by the prophet Daniel).

We are now drawing nearer to the end of the church age (New Testament age). Jesus is still saying Blessed, Blessed, Blessed to those who come to him as poor in spirit, to receive forgiveness for their sins and proclaim Him Lord of their lives.

But He is saying woe! woe! woe! to those who stand in the way of those who would enter the narrow gate that leads to life. He is saying woe! woe! woe! to those self-righteous hypocrites who do the opposite of His gospel as set forth in the Beatitudes. He is saying woe! woe! woe! to those who continue to persecute His prophets in order to save their man-made kingdoms and traditions.

Make no mistake. Before the end of this age, God will make an end to the present man-ordained religious machinery as He did in the last age. Only those houses that are founded on the Rock will stand when the rains come down and the floods rise and the wind beats upon the structures we have built in the name of the Lord.

> See that you do not refuse him that speaks. For if those who refused him that spoke on earth did not escape, much less shall we escape, if we turn away from him that speaks from the heavens, whose voice then shook the earth; but now he has promised, saying, Yet even once, I shall shake not the earth only, but also the heaven. And this word, Yet even once, signifies the removing of those things that are shaken, as of things that are made, that those things which cannot be shaken may remain.
>
> Therefore, receiving a kingdom which cannot be moved, let us hold fast to the grace, by which we serve God, pleasing him with reverence and godly fear: for our God is a consuming fire. (Hebrews 12:25-29).

*Blessed is he that reads and those that hear the words of this prophecy and keep those things which are written therein, for the time is at hand* (Revelation 1:3).

Did you know that there are seven Beatitudes scattered throughout the book of Revelation? Amazingly there is a perfect correlation between them and the Beatitudes of Matthew Chapter 5. I would like to close this book by comparing them for you in the light of the Lord's Prayer (which also has seven parts).

The Beatitudes are the synthesis of the gospel message preached by Jesus Christ. The Lord's Prayer is the response from our hearts that Jesus desires when we hear and receive His message. The Beatitudes of Revelation are a further amplification of the full ramifications of this message. Revelation gives us insight into how God's plan for battle is implemented in the unseen spiritual world and how that impacts the material world we perceive with our five senses.

Recent world events have triggered a flurry of Christian literature on the book of Revelation. Along with increased interest in end time events, it is evident that many believers fear the cataclysmic judgments described in the Apocalypse of John. Too many paranoid Christians spend their time trying to side-step the effects of the curse rather than receiving the blessings of God by faith. The gist of many commentators' interpretations of this book seems to center on complicated theological explanations of how only those who adhere to their doctrine or school of thought will be spared or preserved during the great tribulation and exempted from the great white throne judgment. Since most of these explanations are at odds with one another, the overall effect of this controversy has been to submit the body of Christ to an intense form of intellectual terrorism. We forget that:

> God is charity, and he that abides in charity abides in God, and God in him. In this the charity with us is made perfect, that we may have confidence in the day of judgment, that as he is, so are we in this world. In charity there is no fear; but charity that is perfect casts out fear; because fear has torment; from which he that fears is not complete in charity. We love him, because he first loved us (1 John 4:16-19).

There is a base cause underneath the vicious controversy surrounding the interpretation of end time events. Those whose security is in their doctrines will desperately attack anyone who attempts to present a conflicting view. We must remember that our doctrines cannot save us (even if they are true). In the last chapter we saw that right doctrine alone could not and did not save the scribes and Pharisees. A right relationship with the Lord Jesus Christ (which in turn will bring us into a proper relationship with our brother) is our only hope.

> We love him, because he first loved us. If anyone says, I love God and hates his brother, he is a liar; for he that does not love his brother whom he has seen, how can he love God whom he has not seen? And we have this commandment from him, That he who loves God loves his brother also (1 John 4:19-21).

Jesus Christ is not a terrorist. He is called Faithful and True; with justice He judges and makes war (Rev. 19:11). Those who allow their fears of the future to dictate their eschatology could miss the still small voice of the Lord as He calls everyone to follow Him to the only true place of protection. He Himself is our ark of safety, and He longs to gather us up as a mother hen shelters her chicks under her wings (Matthew 23:37). Will we let Him? Or will we continue to insist on our own man-made doctrines of security. For those who are sheltered in Christ, the seven Beatitudes of Revelation promise hope, rest, protection, eternal satisfaction, freedom from fear, victory over evil with power and authority in the tree of life. Let us set aside our preconceived fears regarding this book and discover the great and glorious promises of God.

The first beatitude:

*Blessed are the poor in spirit, for theirs is the kingdom of the heavens.*

The first line of the Lord's Prayer (Matthew 6:9-13):

*Our Father, who art in the heavens, Hallowed be thy name.*

The first beatitude of Revelation:

*Blessed is he that reads and those that hear the words of this prophecy, and keep those things which are written therein, for the time is at hand* (Revelation 1:3).

We have seen that the only way into the kingdom of heaven is through the narrow gate. We must choose to be poor in spirit and allow God to deal with our pride. We must repent of going our own way and receive forgiveness for our sins. Our own righteousness is as filthy rags before God (Isaiah 64:6). It is His Name and His way that must be hallowed and exalted, not ours. The path to God's blessing begins when we read, hear, and keep the Revelation of Jesus Christ. A mental knowledge of God is not enough. We must take His Revelation to heart if we are to obtain His blessing. Do you have a heart knowledge of Jesus Christ, or only a head knowledge?

The second beatitude:

*Blessed are those that mourn, for they shall be comforted.*

The second line in the Lord's Prayer:

*Thy kingdom come,*

The second beatitude in Revelation:

*And I heard a voice from heaven saying unto me, Write, Blessed are the dead who die in the Lord from now on; Yea, saith the Spirit, that they may rest from their labours, and their works do follow them* (Revelation 14:13).

This beatitude does not only refer to those who have physically died knowing the Lord, it is of supreme importance to those of us still alive. It is the key to obtaining the victory.

*For we are buried with him by baptism into death, that just as the Christ was raised up from the dead to the glory of the Father, likewise we also walk in newness of life. For if we have been planted together in him in the likeness of his death, we shall be also in the likeness of his resurrection, knowing this: that our old man is crucified with him that the body of sin might be destroyed that we should not serve sin any longer* (Romans 6:4-6).

*For the charity of the Christ constrains us because we judge thus: that if one died for all, then all are dead: And that he died for all that those who live should not live from now on unto themselves, but unto him who died and rose again for them* (2 Corinthians 5:14-15).

A lot of water has gone under the bridge between the first and second beatitudes of Revelation. Let me give you a brief summary of these fourteen chapters. A glorious, radiant, all-powerful Jesus Christ has been revealed. His bosom friend, John, took one look at him and fell at Jesus' feet as though dead. This is what we must do as well if we are to receive and transmit to others the revelation of the power, authority, and victory of the risen Savior who holds the keys of death and Hades.

Christ immediately dictated seven letters to John. These letters were addressed to seven specific churches that represent the church at large. The letters are filled with encouragement and exhortation, but sin and apostasy in the church will be judged. Loss of the first love, lukewarmness and hypocrisy will not be tolerated. Those participating in the practices of the Nicolaitans, those who are of the synagogue of Satan, those who hold to the teaching of Baalam, those who tolerate that woman Jezebel, and those who have soiled their clothes ignored God's Word and denied His Name. They will be dealt with directly by Christ. For it is time for judgment to begin from the House of the Lord. (1 Peter 4:17).

Those who overcome in the Name of the Lord are promised the right to eat of the tree of life. They will not be hurt by the second death, and they will be given hidden manna and a new name. They will be given authority over the nations and the morning star, and they will be dressed in white. Their names will never be erased from the Book of Life, and Jesus will acknowledge them before His Father and His Father's angels. They will become pillars in the temple of God with the Name of God, the Name of the new Jerusalem, and Christ's new name written on them. Plus, they will have the right to sit with Jesus Christ on His throne even as Christ sits with His Father on the Father's throne.

The glorious revelation the Father's throne in heaven comes next. Jesus' mission to planet earth was to rescue and redeem creation, bringing everything back into a right relationship with God the Father. In the fall, Adam had signed the title deed of the first creation over to Satan. It was sealed with seven seals, and no one was found worthy to open them, causing great sorrow to John. Through the victory of His death on the cross, the lamb that was slain was found worthy to open the seals, and the legal title of creation was restored to its rightful owner.

The Old Testament concept of redemption was this: if a man sold his land to another (leaving his children without inheritance), his relative or kinsman could pay the price and redeem the property (Leviticus 25:23-28). The mortgage was drawn up on a scroll with the specifications of the land on one side and the signatures on the other side. Then it was sealed. When the kinsman redeemer (such as Boaz in the Book of Ruth) paid off the mortgage, the seals were broken, and the legal title returned to its proper owner. In the case of this earth, however, even though Jesus Christ regained legal title at the cross, Satan, the lawless one, refuses to leave and must be evicted.

As Jesus Christ opens the seals one by one and begins the process of redemption, a great spiritual battle is joined against the kingdom of darkness. God's saints will carry out His plan for battle. The gospel of the kingdom will be preached to all nations, and the earth will be harvested before the end comes. Those who receive the Lord Jesus Christ will ultimately be separated from those who do not. Those who are faithful with little will be given greater responsibility in the age to come.

As the battle rages, God will place His seal on the foreheads of all those who are His. God's seal is the Holy Spirit (Ephesians 1:13). Satan will also place a mark on the hands and foreheads of those who worship him. Those who bear Satan's mark will act and think like he does. They prefer going their own way. They will not obey God. Instead, they will persecute those who wear God's mark. But nothing can touch those who are dead in Christ and sealed by the Holy Spirit. Even if they face physical martyrdom, they will arrive unharmed to the throne of God to rule and reign with Christ. Soon after, a great multitude that no man can number from every nation, tribe, people, and language will stand before the throne in white robes, waving palm branches in their hands.

When the seventh seal of the legal title to creation is opened, Jesus Christ, the rightful owner, will be ready to evict Satan, his hosts of darkness, and all their followers. In response to the prayers of all the saints, the trumpets will sound. The trumpets announce the message: the people of God will set aside their man-made kingdoms and differences of opinion to rally together under the banner of the Lordship and authority of Jesus Christ for the final battle. The children of Israel blew seven trumpets and marched around the walls of Jericho until God brought the enemy walls down. The trumpets will rally the people of God, proclaim the rightful ownership and authority of Christ over everything, and strike fear and terror into the hearts of the enemy.

As the time draws near for the seventh and last trumpet to sound, a powerful angel that coincides perfectly with the glorious description of Jesus Christ in Revelation Chapter 1 will descend to earth from heaven with an open scroll (title deed to the earth) in His hand. He will place His right foot on the sea (the world) and His left foot on the land (the church) (Psalm 95:5). He will take legal possession of the earth with a roar like a lion. Note that Jesus began his work of redemption as the Lamb that was slain, but he will return to claim His possession and evict the enemy with a roar like a lion. The Lamb of God is also the Lion of Judah. Seven thunders will sound, and He will proclaim that there will be no more delay. Soon after, the seventh trumpet will sound.

*The kingdoms of this world are reduced unto our Lord*

*and to his Christ; and he shall reign for ever and ever*
(Revelation 11:15).

John was given revelation from other perspectives such as
measuring the temple of God and the altar. John was allowed
to witness the war in heaven as the dragon (Satan) and his
angels are driven from heaven by Michael and the heavenly
hosts. The dragon and his followers are hurled to earth and
lose no time making war against the saints as they dominate
the world through a many-headed system of control involving
secular power, economic might and false religion.

The dragon's kingdom runs on fear, terror, greed, and
avarice. It will ultimately collapse because a kingdom divided
against itself cannot stand (Matthew 12:25-26). The many-
headed beast, the false prophet, and the great harlot can dominate the world, but they will continually war among themselves.
They all want to go their own way and feed their own selfishness
and pride. The only way poor Satan can hold his shaky empire
together is by force.

*...those that worship the beast and its image and who-*
*soever receives the mark of its name, have no rest day*
*or night* (Revelation 14:11).

If we have turned from our way and set our will to follow
the Lord Jesus Christ, we must renounce the many worldly
pursuits that gave us monetary income, power, prestige, or
pleasure. The apostle James said that friendship with the world
is enmity with God. If we renounce the world to follow Jesus
Christ, we will be comforted. God will send us the Comforter,
His Holy Spirit. It is only by the power and anointing of the
Holy Spirit within us that we can ever hope to do the will of
God here on earth as it is done in heaven.

After we have been emptied of ourselves, God wants to
purify and fill us with Himself. He is to be our righteousness.

We are to be clothed in white garments as we do His will. His Spirit is the Holy Spirit. After we have been divested of our pride in our righteousness, which is as filthy rags before God (Isaiah 64:6), He will cleanse us from the inside out and cover us with Jesus' righteousness. He will clothe us with His Spirit.

When Jesus comes back, everyone will be exposed for what they are. If we have died to ourselves and been crucified with Christ, we are dead to sin and alive through the resurrection power of the Holy Spirit to live for Jesus Christ. Those who are not clothed with the genuine Holy Spirit of Christ will be shamefully exposed when He unexpectedly returns.

*And when the king came in to see the guests, he saw there a man who did not have on a wedding garment, and he said unto him, Friend, how didst thou come in here not having a wedding garment? And he was speechless.*

*Then the king said to the servants, Bind him hand and foot and take him away and cast him into the darkness outside; there shall be weeping and gnashing of teeth. For many are called, but few are chosen* (Matthew 22:11-14).

The system of this world will be destroyed. Everything that can be shaken will be shaken. Revelation speaks of seven vials of the wrath of God that will be poured out to cleanse the earth and bring about the destruction of the beast and his kingdom. But what is darkness and gloom for the children of darkness will be gladness and light for those clothed with the Spirit of God (Joel 3:12-16). When the land of Egypt was devastated by the ten plagues, the land of Goshen (where God's people lived) was unscathed.

*For, behold, the day comes that shall burn as an oven; and all the proud, and all that do wickedly shall be stubble; and the day that comes shall burn them up,*

*said the LORD of the hosts, that it shall leave them nei-
ther root nor branch.*

*But unto you that fear my name shall the Sun of righ-
teousness be born, and in his wings he shall bring saving
health; and ye shall go forth and jump like calves of the
herd. And ye shall tread down the wicked; for they shall
be ashes under the soles of your feet in the day that I
make, said the LORD of the hosts* (Malachi 4:1-3).

Right now, near the end of the church age, we are in the
time of the harvest. The fields are white unto harvest, and the
will of the Lord is to send out laborers to reap the precious
harvest of souls before the end comes. It is imperative that we
be clothed with the Spirit of God so we might inspire hope to
a world that is lost and dying. The world is tired of listening
to the hypocrites representing man-made religion. The ones
our Lord referred to as whitewashed tombs, which outwardly
appear beautiful, but within are full of dead men's bones and
all uncleanness have been unable to keep the gates of Hades
from prevailing against their churches. But the Lord is raising
up a band of overcomers, clothed in His righteousness and led
by His Spirit; they will prevail against the forces of darkness.

The third beatitude:

*Blessed are the meek, for they shall inherit the earth.* The
third line of the Lord's Prayer: *Thy will be done in earth as it
is in heaven.*

The third beatitude from Revelation:

*Behold, I come as a thief. Blessed is he that watches
and keeps his garments lest he walk naked, and they
see his shame* (Revelation 16:15).

The meek are those who submit to the Master. They are like
the horse who can be counted on to willingly obey his master,
even in the heat of battle. The goal of the meek is to see their

Master's kingdom come. This is how they will inherit the earth. But to be victorious, the meek must die to their own way. They must place everything, even their best ideas, possessions, gifts, and abilities on the altar and rest from their (own) labor. Then their deeds (of victorious faith) will follow them. This is what it means to be clothed in fine linen (see Revelation 19:7-8).

The fourth beatitude:

*Blessed are those who hunger and thirst for righteousness, for they shall be satisfied.*

The fourth line of the Lord's Prayer:

*Give us this day our daily bread.*

The fourth beatitude of Revelation:

*And he said unto me, Write, Blessed are those who are called unto the marriage supper of the Lamb. And he said unto me, These are the true words of God* (Revelation 19:9).

Those who are born of God's Spirit, who are born again, find they have different desires and appetites than they had before. They hunger and thirst to please God who promises to fill them with Himself. This is symbolized by the Lord's Supper and speaks of the New Covenant which is Christ in you, the hope of glory.

The Lord's Prayer mentions our daily bread, and the Scripture says *Man shall not live by bread alone, but by every word that proceeds out of the mouth of God* (Luke 4:4). Jesus said *I AM the living bread which came down from heaven; if anyone eats of this bread they shall live forever* (John 6:51). He also said *Unless ye eat the flesh of the Son of man and drink his blood, ye shall have no life in you* (John 6:53).

Those who are invited to the wedding supper of the Lamb will be filled and satisfied in the presence of the Lord for all eternity. They will feed exclusively on the true words of God. Revelation features two women: Christ will return for a bride without spot or wrinkle. On the other hand, Babylon the Great, mother of prostitutes and of all the abominations of the earth, will be destroyed. Abominations are incompatible with the presence of God. The one will exclude the other. The imminent return of Christ precipitates a cataclysmic end on mystery Babylon. God's people are called to come out of her, lest we share in her destruction.

Upon the destruction of Babylon, there will be great joy in heaven. But it is a double celebration. The celebration of the destruction of Babylon will also be the celebration of the wedding supper of the Lamb.

A great multitude in heaven shouts:

> *And again they said, Halelu-JAH. And her smoke rose up for ever and ever. And the twenty-four elders and the four animals fell upon their faces and worshipped God that was seated upon the throne, saying, Amen! Halelu-JAH!*

> *And a voice came out of the throne, saying, Praise our God, all ye his servants and ye that fear him, both small and great. And I heard as it were the voice of a great company and as the voice of many waters and as the voice of mighty thunderings, saying, Halelu-JAH; for the Lord God almighty reigns.*

> *Let us be glad and rejoice and give glory to him; for the marriage of the Lamb is come, and his bride has made herself ready. And to her was granted that she should be arrayed in fine linen, clean and bright: for the fine linen is the righteousness of the saints* (Revelation 19:3-8).

I find a great similarity between this Scripture and the parable of the wheat and the tares.

> *He put forth another parable unto them, saying, The kingdom of the heavens is likened unto a man who sows good seed in his field but while men slept, his enemy came and sowed tares among the wheat and went away. But when the blade was sprung up and brought forth fruit, then the tares appeared also.*
>
> *So the servants of the husband of the house came and said unto him, Lord, didst thou not sow good seed in thy field? from where then does it have tares? He said unto them, The enemy, a man, has done this. The servants said unto him, Wilt thou then that we go and gather them up?*
>
> *But he said, No, lest while ye gather up the tares, ye root up also the wheat with them. Let both grow together until the harvest, and in the time of harvest I will say to the reapers, Gather ye together first the tares and bind them in bundles to burn them, but gather the wheat into my barn.* (Matthew 13:24-30).

Jesus himself was the seed that fell into the ground and died so it might bear fruit in great abundance. His wheat, or church, has been mixed with tares from the beginning of this church age. Notice, however, at harvest time, He is going to gather and burn the tares first and then gather the wheat into His barn.

Listen to Jesus' explanation of this parable:

> *He answered and said unto them, He that sows the good seed is the Son of man; the field is the world; the good seed are the sons of the kingdom, but the tares are the sons of the wicked; and the enemy that sowed them*

*is the devil; the harvest is the end of the age, and the
reapers are the angels.*

*As therefore the tares are gathered and burned in the
fire, so shall it be in the end of this age. The Son of man
shall send forth his angels, and they shall gather out
of his kingdom all things that offend and those who do
iniquity and shall cast them into the furnace of fire;
there shall be wailing and gnashing of teeth. Then shall
the righteous shine forth as the sun in the kingdom
of their Father. He who has ears to hear, let him hear*
(Matthew 13:37-43).

God is getting ready to clean house. He will uproot and
remove all that causes sin and all who do evil from His kingdom
(church). The destruction of Babylon will leave His church without spot or wrinkle, ready for the wedding supper of the Lamb.

The fifth beatitude:

*Blessed are the merciful, for they shall obtain mercy.*

The fifth line of the Lord's Prayer:

*And set us free from our debts, as we set free our
debtors.*

The fifth beatitude in Revelation:

*Blessed and holy is he that has part in the first resur-
rection; on such the second death has no authority, but
they shall be priests of God and of the Christ and shall
reign with him a thousand years* (Revelation 20:6).

Those whom Christ invites to share his throne will be tender channels of His love and mercy. They will heal the broken-
hearted, proclaim liberty to the captives, and open the prison
doors to those who are bound. They will not take advantage of
anyone. No one with a root of bitterness or who is interested in
exacting revenge will be a priest of God or reign with Christ.

Jesus personifies mercy while at the same time He is just, faithful, and true. After He cleanses His church, in His mercy, Jesus will judge the world. The most merciful thing He can do is rid the world of the selfishness, rebellion, and pride that are causing so much pain and sorrow. True mercy is faithful to insist on justice for those unable or unwilling defend themselves. Now Jesus will cleanse the world of those who are filled with extortion and incontinence. He will turn the tables, and some of the last will be first, and some of those who were first will be last.

> *And I saw the heaven open, and behold a white horse; and he that was seated upon him was called Faithful and True, and in righteousness he judges and makes war. And his eyes were as a flame of fire, and on his head were many crowns; and he had a name written, that no one has known, but he himself. And he was clothed with a garment dipped in blood; and his name is called The Word of God.*
>
> *And the armies that are in the heaven followed him upon white horses, clothed in fine linen, white and clean. And out of his mouth goes a sharp sword, that with it he should smite the Gentiles; and he shall rule them with a rod of iron; and he treads the winepress of the fierceness and wrath of Almighty God. And he has on his garment and on his thigh a name written, KING OF KINGS, AND LORD OF LORDS* (Revelation 19:11-16).

The sixth beatitude:

> *Blessed are the pure in heart, for they shall see God.*

The sixth line in the Lord's Prayer:

> *And lead us not into temptation, but deliver us from evil,*

The sixth beatitude in Revelation:

*Behold, I come quickly; blessed is he that keeps the*
*words of the prophecy of this book* (Revelation 22:7).

The pure in heart are full of integrity. They are empty of themselves and overflowing with the Holy Spirit. Springs of living water flow from their soul. They project God's peace. They are the only ones who will be able to keep the words of the prophecy of this book. (The word for book, *Biblion*, is the root for our term Bible.) Only the pure in heart can stand against the temptations of the evil one. Only the pure in heart can live a life that will measure up to the standards of God's Word. Only one person has a pure heart, and that is Jesus. He wants to live in us and give us His heart. We are the temple of God.

The pure in heart will see God face to face. Satan will be dealt with, and the dead will be judged. Everything will be made new! There will be a new heaven and a new earth. The New Jerusalem, the bride of Christ, will come down from heaven. The abode of God will be among men.

*And there shall in no wise enter into it anything*
*unclean or that works abomination or makes a lie, but*
*only those who are written in the Lamb's book of life.*

*And he showed me a pure river of water of life, clear*
*as crystal, proceeding out of the throne of God and*
*of the Lamb. In the midst of her plaza and on either*
*side of the river was the tree of life, which brings*
*forth twelve manner of fruits, yielding her fruit every*
*month; and the leaves of the tree are for the healing of*
*the Gentiles. And there shall no longer be any cursed*
*thing* (Revelation 21:27-22:3).

This is the end result of the Beatitudes. The river of life flows from God's throne. Redeemed and regenerate humanity will regain access to the tree of life, and the healing of the nations will follow. God's blessing will overcome the curse. God's battle plan will succeed in overcoming the enemy, and an eternity of peace is on the horizon. Contrast this with our modern cities that generate pollution, misery and despair.

> And there shall no longer be any cursed thing; but the throne of God and of the Lamb shall be in her; and his servants shall serve him; and they shall see his face; and his name shall be in their foreheads. And there shall be no night there; and they need no lamp neither light of the sun; for the Lord God shall give them light; and they shall reign for ever and ever (Revelation 22:3-5).

The seventh beatitude:

> Blessed are the peacemakers, for they shall be called the sons of God.

The seventh line of the Lord's Prayer:

> For thine is the kingdom and the power and the glory forever. Amen.

The seventh beatitude in Revelation:

> Blessed are those who do his commandments that their power and authority might be in the tree of life and they may enter in through the gates into the city (Revelation 22:14).

The sons of God shall inherit the kingdom. They are joint heirs with Jesus Christ. Our robes must be washed in the blood of the Lamb. We must die daily to our own plans and ambitions and live for Him if we are to have power and authority in the tree of life and be able to administer God's peace to those who do not have it.

> But outside are the dogs and the sorcerers and the fornicators and the murderers and the idolaters and whosoever loves and makes a lie. I, Jesus, have sent my angel to testify unto you these things in the churches. I

*AM the root and the offspring of David and the bright and morning star.*

*And the Spirit and the bride say, Come. And let him that hears say, Come. And let him that is thirsty come; and whosoever will, let him take of the water of life freely* (Revelation 22:15-17).

# About the Author

At the age of four, while his family was living in Minneapolis, Minnesota, Russell Stendal prayed and asked God to call his parents, Chad and Pat, to be missionaries. God answered that prayer and within just a few years the whole family was on the mission field in Colombia, South America. He became an accomplished jungle pilot and married a beautiful Colombian lady named Marina. They have four children, Lisa, Alethia, Russell Jr., and Dylan, plus six grandchildren.

When Russell was 27 years old, Marxist guerrillas of the FARC kidnapped him for 142 days. The story of his kidnapping is told in the book he wrote titled Rescue the Captors. His reason for the title is because he realized that his captors were more captive than he was. There was a possibility he would be released, but most of his kidnappers were young people who had been taken from their families, given a weapon, and taught to kill. They had little hope of survival.

To reach all the actors of the armed conflict, including his former captors, Russell established a radio ministry to air programs into the dangerous war stricken areas of Colombia with messages of peace and hope. He has also written more than 50 books in English and Spanish.

In 2017, he was awarded the Shahbaz Bhatti Freedom Award, (given to Pope Francis the year before) for his tireless efforts towards spreading peace and reconciliation in Colombia (in the context of promoting religious freedom). Russell travels extensively as a guest speaker in conventions around the world. His speaking is unique in that he is very sensitive to the Lord's voice and does not hesitate to deliver the message imparted to him, no matter how uncomfortable that may be to him or to others. Most of the books he has published were transcribed directly from the radio messages he has preached in Spanish and beamed into virtually all of the war torn areas of the countryside.

Russell is the editor of the Jubilee Bible translation that has been published in English and in Spanish. Well over a million copies of this Bible have been donated and distributed into the most needy areas of Colombia and Venezuela.

# Connect with the Stendal's Ministry

For more information on the Stendals Ministry, and to find out the latest news on how to pray for Colombia visit the following websites:

## Website

www.cpcsociety.ca

www.spiritofmartyrdom.com/

## Receive newsletter updates

https://spiritofmartyrdom.com/application-form/ (Check the Latin America box to get the latest newsletter on the Stendal's Ministry)

## Buy books

http://amzn.to/1nPLcNL

Manufactured by Amazon.ca
Bolton, ON

32938394R00129